# VEDANTA
## BOOK OF DEFINITIONS
## *Tattvabodha*

of
Śrī Ādi Śaṅkarācārya

Commentary by
**Swami Tejomayananda**

Central Chinmaya Mission Trust

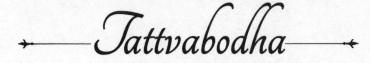

First Printed in the United states of America
In India, Printed upto September 2011 – 27,000 copies
Revised Edition – July 2016 – 12,000 copies
Reprint – August 2017 – 3,000 copies

Published by:
**Chinmaya Prakashan**
The Publications Division of
**Central Chinmaya Mission Trust**
Sandeepany Sadhanalaya
Saki Vihar Road, Powai, Mumbai 400072, India
Tel.: +91-22-2857 2367, 2857 5806 • Fax: +91-22-2857 3065
Email: ccmtpublications@chinmayamission.com
Website: www.chinmayamission.com

Distribution Centre in USA:
**Chinmaya Mission West**
Publications Division
560 Bridgetown Pike, Langhorne, PA 19053, USA
Tel.: 1-888-CMW-READ, (215) 396-0390 • Fax: (215) 396-9710
Email: publications@chinmayamission.org
Website: www.chinmayapublications.org

Designed by: Chinmaya Kalpanam, Mumbai

Printed by: Usha Multigraphs Pvt. Ltd., Mumbai

ISBN 978-81-7597-561-3

# CONTENTS

## Transliteration and Pronunciation Guide

In the book, Devanāgarī characters are transliterated according to the scheme adopted by the International Congress of Orientalists at Athens in 1912. In it one fixed pronunciation value is given to each letter; f, q, w, x and z are not called to use.

| Devanāgarī | Translit-eration | Sounds Like | Devanāgarī | Translit-eration | Sounds Like |
|---|---|---|---|---|---|
| अ | a | son | ढ् | ḍh | adhesive* |
| आ | ā | father | ण् | ṇ | under* |
| इ | i | different | त् | t | tabla |
| ई | ī | feel | थ् | th | thumb |
| उ | u | full | द् | d | this |
| ऊ | ū | boot | ध् | dh | Gandhi |
| ऋ | ṛ | rhythm* | न् | n | nose |
| ॠ | ṝ | ** | प् | p | pen |
| ऌ | ḷ | ** | फ् | ph | phantom* |
| ए | e | evade | ब् | b | boil |
| ऐ | ai | delight | भ् | bh | abhor |
| ओ | o | core | म् | m | mind |
| औ | au | now | य् | y | yes |
| क् | k | calm | र् | r | right |
| ख् | kh | khan | ल् | l | love |
| ग् | g | gate | व् | v | very |
| घ् | gh | ghost | श् | ś | shut |
| ङ् | ṅ | ankle* | ष | ṣ | sugar |
| च् | c | chuckle | स् | s | simple |
| छ् | ch | witch* | ह् | h | happy |
| ज् | j | justice | ं | ṁ | improvise |
| झ् | jh | Jhansi | ः | ḥ | ** |
| ञ् | ñ | banyan | क्ष् | kṣ | action |
| ट् | ṭ | tank | त्र् | tr | three* |
| ठ् | ṭh | ** | ज्ञ् | jñ | gnosis |
| ड् | ḍ | dog | ऽ | ʼ | a silent 'a' |

* These letters don't have an exact English equivalent. An approximation is given here.

** These sounds cannot be approximated in English words.

# Introduction

Vedānta begins with the question – what is the goal of human life? Each one of us seem to have an apparently different goal. One wants to become a doctor, another an actor, and yet another an Olympic gold medallist, and almost all of us want to become rich. If asked, "Why do you want to become a doctor or an actor? Why do you want money or fame?" The final answer is, "To become happy". So, in and through all our pursuits we desire happiness alone. This is the common goal of all living beings. We think happiness is in 'this' or 'that' object and so we make the object our goal.

When did this desire for happiness begin in us? We find that we are born with it. The search for happiness presupposes an existing state of dissatisfaction or sorrow. Is it not strange that all human beings have been searching since beginningless time, from morning to night, birth to death, life after life, for happiness and yet they do not seem to have found it? Could we not give up this desire and remain in sorrow? That too, is not possible. We cannot be happy being unhappy!

Let us enquire, what is the nature of the happiness that we seek? Do we want to be happy today, tomorrow or next year? No. We want to be happy every moment, starting from now, and forever after. Hence, all fairy tales end with the sentence 'And they lived happily ever after'. We seek eternal happiness. If we experience some happiness in place/object/situation/person 'A' and some more in 'B', then, we seek 'B' because we want the maximum possible happiness. In fact, we want unlimited, infinite, eternal happiness.

Presently, we seek to change the following, in order to gain happiness, but do we find it?

a) **Place :** We undergo lots of travails in travel to reach a holiday resort. When the novelty of the place wears out or we run out of money we return.

b) **Time :** We always wait for better times to come.

c) **Objects :** We change our cars, houses and TVs with regularity, hoping that the new model will give us greater joy or lesser trouble.

d) **Circumstances/Status :** The bachelor wants to get married, the married one divorces and yet another becomes a renunciate, in order to become happy. We change jobs in search of job satisfaction, to often find that we have jumped from the frying pan into the fire.

e) **People :** We make and break human relations. We fire the maid in order to make the mother happy, and ask her to leave in order to keep the wife smiling!

f) **Body :** We have evolved over innumerable lives from the unicellular organism to the human, just to be happy. But even in this life, many contemplate suicide, in other words, change the body to get rid of sorrow.

So, just by changing the above, our desire for happiness does not end. It would only end when we gain eternal infinite Bliss. Where is this happiness that we seek located? Are we looking for it in the wrong place?

There are two aspects to life: 'I' the experiencer, the subject, and the world of objects, emotions and thoughts. Now let us ascertain if happiness is the nature of the subject or of the objects. One cannot say that there is nothing called happiness, since we all experience it – however fleetingly. Sweetness is the nature of sugar; hence every particle of it is sweet. Irrespective of the time, place, circumstances and the person who eats it, it tastes sweet. If eaten for the fiftieth time, it would still taste sweet. Similarly, if happiness were the nature of the objects of the world, irrespective of the one who experiences them, when, where or however frequently, they would give us joy. For example, chocolates seem to give joy to many. But if we were woken up at midnight to eat one, what would be our reaction? The fiftieth bar of chocolate would make us sick. This enquiry should be done by each one of us about all the objects of the world. If happiness is not the nature of any object, then by the law of the remainder (pariśeṣa nyāya), it should be the nature of the subject. Therefore, I am the source of happiness. In fact, I am infinite Bliss. I am what I seek. This is the essence of the Vedas, the revelations of the great sages (ṛṣis).

Let us think further in order to ascertain this fact which may initially seem too farfetched. In the deep sleep state, there is no world, yet we experience happiness. Therefore, it is wrong to think that objects alone make us happy. Who is it that experiences happiness in deep sleep? I am there to witness the state of sleep and be happy.

Everything tends to change or go towards its own inherent nature. For example, if a block of ice is placed at room temperature, it begins to melt and continues to do so till it has fully reached its most natural state, water. What is it that we go towards, joy or sorrow? Our own nature is never a burden to us. Is happiness ever considered a burden? We only get weighed down by sorrow, never by happiness. Hence, unconditioned objectless happiness is our own true nature.

There are two types of achievements in the world:

a) Gain of the ungained thing (aprāptasya prāptiḥ): Assuming that I am a pauper and in need of money, I have to know how to make money and then work hard to gain it. Therefore, knowledge + action = gain.

b) Gain of the thing already gained (prāptasya prāptiḥ): If I were to search for my lost keys and someone points out that they were in my pocket all along, do I have to do anything to gain them? No! They were always with me, but through ignorance I thought I had lost them. On knowing about their whereabouts, I 'gained' them. Therefore, knowledge = gain. No action is required.

The gain of the Self obviously belongs to the second category. The Self is never far from us in terms of time or place. Happiness only appears ungained due to the ignorance of the Self. It can be gained by Self-knowledge.

For any knowledge to take place, three factors are required:

a) The object to be known (prameya)

b) The knower of the object (pramātā)

c) The means of knowing it (pramāṇa)

The most common means of knowledge are:

a) **Direct perception** (pratyakṣa pramāṇa): It is the knowledge gained through the five sense organs of perception. For example, eyes see colour and form.

b) **Inference** (anumāna pramāṇa): Based on what we perceive and already know, we infer a thing. For example, we have experienced that wherever there is smoke, there is fire. Therefore, on seeing smoke, we can infer that there must be fire.

c) **Words or verbal testimony** (śabda pramāṇa): We gain knowledge by reading or hearing from people who have directly experienced a thing or heard about it. Both inference and word knowledge, are based on direct perception.

As regards Self-knowledge, the object to be known (prameya) is the Self and the knower (pramātā) is also the Self. What is the means of gaining it? The Self is not available for direct perception, therefore, it cannot be inferred or spoken of. Then how is Self-knowledge possible? The means for it is the Vedas.

The Vedas are the discoveries of the truths or laws of nature, the world, the beings living in it and the ultimate

Truth. They are called 'apauruṣeya grantha' – works not authored by any human being. They are not books composed by men at a particular period in history. Like the discovery of the law of gravitation by Newton, the ancient Masters received these eternal truths as revelations in meditation. They were later compiled and codified by sage Veda-vyāsa into the four Vedas *(Ṛg-veda, Yajur-veda, Sāma-veda, Atharva-veda).*

The main topics of the Vedas are:

a) **Dharma:** The laws governing the individual (jīva), the world (jagat) and the Creator (Īśvara), their inter-relationship, the laws of karma and so on, by which man can lead a successful worldly life. This part of the Vedas is called Karma-kāṇḍa and Upāsanā-kāṇḍa.

b) **Brahman:** The knowledge of the ultimate Truth/Self-knowledge. It answers the fundamental questions of life like 'Who am 'I'? and What is my goal in life?' It liberates individuals from the limitations of worldly existence. This portion is called Jñāna-kāṇḍa, Upaniṣad or Vedānta.

The three basic texts that a student of Vedānta studies from a Guru are the Upaniṣads, *Brahma-sūtras* and the *Bhagavad-gītā*. They are called the 'Prasthāna Trayī'. The new initiates, if they were to begin with these texts right away, would find them difficult to comprehend, and therefore, they are first taught introductory texts (prakaraṇa granthaḥ). These books explain the basic concepts of Vedānta in simple terms, without going into any argumentation of various philosophic thoughts.

*Tattvabodha,* authored by Ādi Śaṅkarācārya, is an introductory text which expounds the essence of Vedānta and its terminology in a simple question-answer style (prakaraṇa granthaḥ). The commentary is meant to further simplify our study.

# Invocation

An auspicious beginning foretells an auspicious end. So, all spiritual texts begin with an invocatory prayer in which we invoke the grace of the Lord and the Guru. It is only due to His grace that the writing, speaking, listening or reading of any text is possible and with His grace alone would the text reach its culmination, its ultimate purpose being the realisation of the Truth. Prayer fills the heart with humility, love and strength. It inspires us and opens the doors of our inherent creative potential. Śrī Śaṅkarācārya – true to tradition of Vedānta, starts the text with an invocatory prayer.

वासुदेवेन्द्रयोगीन्द्रं नत्वा ज्ञानप्रदं गुरुम् ।
मुमुक्षूणां हितार्थाय तत्त्वबोधोऽभिधीयते ।।

*vāsudevendra-yogīndraṁ natvā jñānapradaṁ gurum,*
*mumukṣūṇāṁ hitārthāya tattvabodho'bhidhīyate.*

वासुदेवेन्द्रयोगीन्द्रं – Vāsudevendra, the king amongst yogīs; नत्वा – having saluted; ज्ञानप्रदं – the bestower of knowledge; गुरुम् – Guru; मुमुक्षूणां – of the seekers; हितार्थाय – for the benefit; तत्त्वबोध: – *Tattvabodhaḥ*; अभिधीयते – is expounded

Having saluted Śrī Vāsudevendra, the king of yogīs, the Guru, who is the bestower of knowledge, *Tattvabodha* is expounded for the benefit of the seekers.

**Vāsudevendra:** The Consciousness pulsating within each of us incarnated as Śrī Kṛṣṇa, the son of Vasudeva and Devakī, due to the demand of the age.

**Yogīndra:** A yogī is one who practises yoga (not necessarily as in Aṣṭāṅga-yoga). The king of yogīs is the one who has attained yoga, union with the Self. Lord Śrī Kṛṣṇa is the king of all practitioners of yoga and those who have attained yoga.

**Jñānapradaṁ gurum:** The Guru is the one who removes the darkness of ignorance with the light of knowledge. (gu = darkness + ru = remover). Lord Kṛṣṇa is worshipped as the Guru of all, as all knowledge originates from the Lord alone. (Kṛṣṇaṁ vande jagad-guruṁ).

One of the names of Lord Kṛṣṇa is Govinda. Śaṅkarācārya's Guru was also called Govindapādācārya. So in this verse, along with the Lord Śrī Kṛṣṇa, Śaṅkarācārya also salutes his own Teacher, the king among yogīs and the giver of Self-knowledge.

In the spiritual tradition of India, authors of texts followed the convention of proving right at the beginning the purpose of writing a book. The book would not be accepted if written without a valid reason. In modern school texts, we find that the subject and the student group for whom it is meant, is specified on the cover itself. For example, Geography for Standard 5. In this manner, the texts are readily identifiable. In the past too, authors used to present such specifications, technically called 'anubandha catuṣṭaya', which comprises of the following:

a) For whom the text is meant (adhikārī): *Tattvabodha* is meant for the seeker of Liberation (mumukṣūṇāṃ). One who wants name, fame, pleasures and power need not waste time reading this text. Those who want to free themselves of all limitations and sorrows for all times to come, are fit for this knowledge.

b) The subject matter of the text (viṣaya): 'That' without which a thing is not itself or in other words, the essence or Reality is called tattva; tat = 'that', tva = 'ness'; bodha means knowledge. Tattvabodha is the knowledge of the Reality, the subject of the text.

c) The purpose of the text (prayojana): The purpose of *Tattvabodha* is Liberation. Man seeks several means of getting rid of his many sorrows. They may be temporarily alleviated, but they never end for good. Man wants to be permanently free from sorrow. This is possible only through the knowledge of Reality.

d) The relation of the text to the purpose (sambandha): By the study of *Tattvabodha* and the realisation of the Truth, the seeker of liberation gains Liberation. This is called relation of the revealed and the revealer. (bodhya-bodhaka-sambandha).

Thus the invocatory verse not only invokes the grace of the Lord and the Guru, but also indicates the anubandha catuṣṭaya.

***

The topic is introduced with:

साधनचतुष्टयसंपन्नाधिकारिणां मोक्षसाधनभूतं
तत्त्वविवेकप्रकारं वक्ष्यामः।

*sādhana-catuṣṭaya-sampannādhikāriṇāṁ mokṣa-sādhanabhūtaṁ tattvaviveka-prakāraṁ vakṣyāmaḥ.*

साधनचतुष्टय-संपन्नाधिकारिणां – for those who are endowed with the fourfold qualifications; मोक्षसाधनभूतं – the means of liberation; तत्त्वविवेकप्रकारं – the mode of enquiry into the nature of the Reality; वक्ष्यामः – we shall expound

We shall explain to those who are endowed with the fourfold qualifications, the mode of enquiry into the Reality, which is the means of Liberation.

The mode of discrimination or enquiry: The word 'viveka' comes from the verbal root 'vic' meaning to separate. Man has the subtle power of discrimination that distinguishes him from other beings. In the state of ignorance, he uses it merely to recognise objects and concepts of the world; comparing, contrasting and categorising them or distinguishing between the conducive and the non-conducive. For example, this is good music, or the brown shirt is better than the blue one. When this same faculty is used for discriminating the Real from the unreal, it liberates man.

The means of Liberation: All bondage is due to either total lack of thinking, incomplete thinking or wrong thinking. It can be removed by right and complete thinking. (avicāra kṛto bandhaḥ vicāreṇa nivartate). It is said that most problems would not arise if only we paused to think for a moment, but a moment is a long time and thinking is a difficult process! We all think from morning to night and from birth to death. But the question is, do we really think? Most of the times thinking just happens. Uncontrolled, irrelevant, dissociated and distracted thoughts occur at random and then, this thinking leads to worry, anger, tension and quarrels.

Now, for a change, let us think differently, let us think about the fundamental questions of life like 'Who am I?' 'Am I the ever-changing body and the fluctuating mind? What is the goal of my life? Is it merely to eat, drink and be merry?' This enquiry is the means to liberate us from all conflicts of life.

When we are endowed with the fourfold qualifications, we can liberate ourselves by means of right enquiry. But we are unable to conduct it, due to our own inadequacy. The mind is not subtle, pure or single pointed enough to delve deep. One who has the fourfold qualifications is capable of enquiry and realisation, just as one who has completed a Master's degree in physics is qualified for attempting a Doctorate in that field.

# The Fourfold Qualification

साधनचतुष्टयं किम्? नित्यानित्यवस्तुविवेकः ।
इहामुत्रार्थफलभोगविरागः। शमादिषट्कसंपत्तिः ।
मुमुक्षुत्वं चेति।।

*sādhana-catuṣṭayaṁ kim? nityānityavastu-vivekaḥ, ihāmutrārthaphalabhoga-virāgaḥ, śamādiṣaṭka-saṁpattiḥ, mumukṣutvaṁ ceti.*

साधनचतुष्टयं – fourfold qualification; किम् – what; नित्यानित्यवस्तुविवेकः – discrimination between the permanent and the impermanent; इहामुत्रार्थफलभोगविरागः – dispassion towards the enjoyment of the fruits of actions here and hereafter; शमादिषट्कसंपत्तिः – the sixfold wealth like śama etc; मुमुक्षुत्वं – yearning for Liberation; च – and; इति – thus

What is the fourfold qualification? The capacity to discriminate between the permanent and the impermanent, dispassion towards the enjoyment of the fruits of one's actions here and hereafter, the group of six accomplishments (inner wealth) beginning with śama and the yearning for Liberation.

***

After enumerating the fourfold qualifications, each is elaborated upon.

**Discrimination:**

नित्यानित्यवस्तुविवेकः कः?
नित्यवस्त्वेकं ब्रह्म तद्व्यतिरिक्तं सर्वमनित्यम्।
अयमेव नित्यानित्यवस्तुविवेकः।।

*nityānityavastu-vivekaḥ kaḥ?*
*nityavastvekaṁ brahma tad-vyatiriktaṁ sarvam-anityam,*
*ayameva nityānityavastu-vivekaḥ.*

नित्यानित्यवस्तुविवेकः – discrimination between the permanent and the impermanent; कः – what; नित्यवस्तु – the eternal; एकं – alone; ब्रह्म – the Reality; तद्व्यतिरिक्तं – apart from It; सर्वम् – all; अनित्यम् – are ephemeral; अयम् – this; एव – alone; नित्यानित्यवस्तुविवेकः – discrimination between the permanent and the impermanent

What is meant by discrimination between the permanent and the impermanent? The Reality alone is eternal; everything else is ephemeral. This conviction alone is the discrimination between the permanent and the impermanent.

Viveka is the capacity of the intellect to distinguish, categorise and recognise one thing from another. This is present even in animals. They separate the edible from the inedible and a friend from a foe. But only man can use this faculty to enquire into the relationship between the part and the whole (aṁśa-aṁśī-viveka), the means and the goal (sādhana-sādhya-viveka), the good and the pleasant (śreya-preya-viveka), the Self and the not-Self (ātma-anātmaviveka), the eternal and the ephemeral (nitya-anitya-viveka) and so on.

Most of us use this faculty to distinguish between two perishable objects (anitya-anitya-viveka). One desiring Liberation should have a well-developed capacity to discriminate between the eternal and ephemeral (nitya-anitya-viveka).

On enquiry, we realise that the only constant thing, the only changeless thing in the world is that everything changes. The size and the weight of the body changes, the hair greys, the moods of the mind change, our intellectual capacities and opinions change, personalities change, duties change, faith changes and so on. The objects and beings around us change, relationships change and so do the economic, political and social circumstances. Education, technology, fashions, lifestyles, modes of transport and communication, entertainment... everything is changing. The earth and the elements, the rivers and mountains and even the sun, moon, the stars and their configurations change. From the subatomic to the cosmic level, everything is in a state of flux. Things come and go, staying only for a little while. Nothing lasts forever, however much we may want it to.

Is there not anything permanent? Sure, there is. For every change, there must be a changeless substratum. The changing factors are innumerable, but the changeless cannot be many. It must be one alone and being beyond time, must be Eternal. This eternal factor is called Brahman, the Reality in scriptures. It is only when one intensely realises the changing nature of everything that the changeless Reality can be distinguished from all else. This firm determination of what changes and what does not is called 'nityānitya vastu viveka', the first of the fourfold qualifications.

***

**Dispassion:**

विरागः कः? इहस्वर्गभोगेषु इच्छाराहित्यम्।।

*virāgaḥ kaḥ? ihasvarga-bhogeṣu icchārāhityam.*

विरागः – dispassion; कः – what; इहस्वर्गभोगेषु – the enjoyments in this world and heaven; इच्छाराहित्यम् – lack of desire

What is dispassion? The absence of desire for the enjoyments (of the fruits of one's actions) in this world and in heaven.

People fear the word 'dispassion'. They feel that they have to give up their spouse and children and all the pleasures of life, to gain dispassion. Dispassion does not imply running away from society or hating it and criticising its enjoyments. It is also not the apparent disinterest that one shows when the object is not available (alābhe vairāgya) or forbidden like the diabetic's show of indifference towards sweets. It is not the temporary lack of interest that one feels towards pleasures on the death of a dear one (smaśāna vairāgya).

Man runs after objects thinking that they give joy. By objects is also implied persons and situations. He is temporarily happy when he gains them and unhappy when he does not. His craving increases as also his dependence on the object. When he has determined the sorrowful and impermanent nature of objects, he stops craving for them. When he realises that joy is not in objects, he loses interest in them (audāsīnyaṁ). When he knows that true joy is in the nature of the eternal Reality within, then there is total dispassion for every object, worldly or heavenly.

As long as one feels that objects have joy, one cannot but have likes or dislikes for them. One has to repeatedly reflect on the nature of objects to determine firmly that they have no joy[1] as the mind tends to superimpose joy either on the same or different objects. Every smoker knows and also experiences, that cigarette smoking is injurious to health. Yet most are unable to give up smoking.

Dispassion therefore, is the strength to give up the sorrow giving, impermanent and joyless objects, mentally or physically. It is the absence of both like or dislike for objects. We have dispassion for particular objects, but crave for certain others. For example, many are disinterested in the joys available in their motherland, but crave for a higher standard of living elsewhere. One with total dispassion does not desire even the subtlest pleasures of the heavens. *Kaṭhopaniṣad* relates how young Naciketas shunned all heavenly pleasures, when Lord Yama offered them to him.

Dispassion arises from discrimination. Dispassion purifies the mind and makes one capable of subtler

[1] manasi vicintaya vāraṁ vāram – *Bhaja Govindam*-3.

discrimination. Hence, dispassion increases discrimination and vice versa. Dispassion also arises out of the choiceless yet dedicated performance of one's duties (dharma te virati). Also, when actions are performed as a dedicated service to the Lord, likes and dislikes decrease and dispassion increases.

One with dispassion is fearless (vairāgyam eva abhayam) as he does not depend upon anything for his joy. He is peaceful and cheerful, irrespective of the presence or absence of objects of enjoyment. The man with passion lives for his own pleasure; whereas one with dispassion truly loves and serves others.

Discrimination and dispassion are the two wings on which the seeker flies towards the Truth.

***

**The Sixfold Wealth:**

शमादिसाधनसंपत्तिः का?
शमो दम उपरतिस्तितिक्षा श्रद्धा समाधानं च इति ।।

*śamādisādhana-saṁpattiḥ kā?*
*śamo dama uparatistitikṣā śraddhā samādhānaṁ ca iti.*

शमादिसाधनसंपत्तिः – the inner wealth starting with mind control; का – what; शमः – mind control; दमः – control of senses; उपरतिः – withdrawal of the mind; तितिक्षा – forbearance; श्रद्धा – faith; समाधानम् – absorption of the mind; च – and; इति – thus

What is the inner wealth starting with śama? They are control on the mind, control of the senses, withdrawal of the mind, forbearance, faith and absorption of the mind.

The light of dawn precedes the rising of the sun. It dispels the darkness and beautifies the world. Similarly, the sixfold inner wealth beautifies our personalities and behaviour even before the rise of the knowledge of the Truth. Outer wealth decreases on spending and can increase our sorrow. Inner wealth increases with use and decreases our grief. The six are interrelated and the seeker needs to equip himself with all of them for his spiritual progress.

***

**Control of the mind:**

शमः कः? मनोनिग्रहः।।

*śamaḥ kaḥ? manonigrahaḥ.*

शमः – śama; कः – what; मनोनिग्रहः – mind control

What is śama? It is control or mastery over the mind.

The mind is a continuous flow of thoughts. The thoughts, innumerable in number, are about various objects and flash in and out of the mind at high speed. Each thought by itself appears flimsy, but the total force of the mind is terrific. It prompts us into various actions. It becomes agitated, distracted, is stubborn and unyielding[1].

[1] cañcalaṁ hi manaḥ kṛṣṇa pramāthi balavad dṛḍham – *Gītā*-6.34

We may disobey others, but we are enslaved by our own mind. The moods of the mind toss us from elation to depression; from the sublime to the ridiculous. One who possesses such a mind cannot undertake any enquiry into the nature of oneself.

A man sitting in a room goes out due to either of the two reasons: (a) Someone from outside calls him, or (b) He is bored and his mind desires something and prompts him to go out. Similarly, man gets distracted due to: (a) The senses that run after the objects and prompt the mind to run along with them and (b) Inner desires or memories that prompt the mind into the world of objects.

When we refuse to react, participate or entertain these distracting thoughts, they lose their hold over us and we remain in full control of the mind. This requires alertness and continuous vigilance. We can also control the mind by withdrawing it from objects by understanding their sorrow giving and desire prompting nature (doṣa dṛṣṭyā muhurmuhuḥ). We have to break the habit of the mind, of remaining preoccupied with thoughts and brooding over objects. The mind may not take too kindly to this disciplining, but by intelligent practice, not force, it turns out to be our best friend. One who has controlled one's mind, has as well, controlled the world.

***

**Control of the Senses:**

दमः कः? चक्षुरादि बाह्येन्द्रियनिग्रहः।।

*damaḥ kaḥ? cakṣurādi-bāhyendriya-nigrahaḥ.*

दमः – dama; कः – what; चक्षुरादि – eyes, etc; बाह्येन्द्रियनिग्रहः – control of the external senses

What is dama? It is the control of the external sense organs such as the eyes.

To the one with control over the mind (śama), control over the senses (dama) is natural. But when one loses control over the mind, yet retains control over the senses, that is dama. For example, one may get angry, but refrain from using harsh words.

The senses are extrovert by nature. Like wild horses they run after their respective sense objects simultaneously or sequentially, but continuously, never allowing the mind to remain at peace. The tongue wants to taste spicy food or keep on talking; the eyes want to watch TV; the hands are restless and so on. The senses thus do not discriminate between the good and the pleasant, but entertain the mind with the unwanted and unhealthy perceptions.

The process of training the senses (just as we tame horses) is called dama. A life of discipline and healthy habits helps to control the senses. One must train the senses to follow good habits or exercise control, even when provoked or tempted. For example, a well brought up child would not use bad words, even when provoked, as he may never have been exposed to them. Or he may even know them, but still not resort to saying them.

If the senses are controlled by force or fear, the mind revolts or keeps brooding over pleasures. Many people keep thinking more of food on the days they observe fasting, which is perhaps why some feast the day after they fast! Control of the senses (dama) should aid control of the mind (śama) and vice versa.

***

**Withdrawal of the Mind:**

उपरमः कः? स्वधर्मानुष्ठानमेव ।।

*uparamaḥ kaḥ? svadharmānuṣṭhānameva.*

उपरमः – uparamaḥ; कः – what; स्वधर्मानुष्ठानम् – observance of one's own dharma; एव – alone

What is uparama or uparati (as it is also known)? It is the strict observance of one own's dharma (duty).

It is the state of the mind and senses that has withdrawn from revelling in the world of objects (upa + rama = uparama). When control of the mind and the senses become natural, withdrawal of the mind is automatically achieved. In śama and dama the mind and senses may be amongst objects, but are restrained with alertness, but in uparama they automatically withdraw from objects. The example given in the *Gītā* is of the tortoise that withdraws its head and limbs effortlessly into its shell, when in danger.

Śrī Śaṅkarācārya defines it as the strict observance of one's own duties. Duties come to all of us according to our age, position and place in life. Many of us revolt against its performance, or do so out of habit or force, often bored and burdened by them. A student dislikes studies and goes to school as though to oblige his parents. But when one's duties are performed with enthusiasm and dedication, not only does the performance bring joy, but the mind also becomes steady, single pointed, free of likes and dislikes, peaceful and withdrawn. The highest form of uparama is when one remains in one's ultimate and true nature (svadharma), which is Existence-Consciousness-Bliss. Outer withdrawal and performance of one's duty are necessary to reach that state.

***

**Forbearance:**

तितिक्षा का? शीतोष्णसुखदुःखादिसहिष्णुत्वम्।।

*titikṣā kā? śitoṣṇa-sukhaduḥkhādi-sahiṣṇutvam.*

तितिक्षा – titikṣā; का – what; शीत–उष्ण–सुख–दुःखादि–सहिष्णुत्वम् – endurance of heat, cold, joy, sorrow, etc.

What is titikṣā? It is the endurance of heat and cold, pleasure and pain, etc.

The world gives us a continuous stream of experiences at the physical level (heat, cold, etc.), emotional level (joy, sorrow, etc.) and intellectual level (praise, censure, etc.), that may be conducive or non-conducive; more often non-conducive. When confronted with non-conducive situations, we normally complain or blame others. Some curse the Lord, the government, society, family or one's own destiny. Many get dejected, depressed or upset. Some revolt, get angry and fight back. They say, "Bhagavān seems to have only my address for sending me packets of sorrow" or "I wish I was born rich; then I would not have to undergo this trouble" or "Everyone is after my blood. Why does it happen only to me? Nothing will ever work out right for me. My stars are not in the right place" or "All my problems are because of you, I shall get back at you for this insult" or "I am a born loser". However one may react, one has to go through the situation. There is no choice in that. The only choice lies in the attitude with which we go through it.

To be able to bear non-conducive situations without reacting, complaining or blaming, but with a cheerful acceptance, is called titikṣā[1]. When a certain saint was abused, he calmly said, "I already know I am like that! Don't you have anything to say about me that I am not aware of?"

When one travels in a vehicle that has good shock absorbers, the ride is smooth, even if the road is bad. Titikṣā is the shock absorber with which one rides the rough terrain of life without breaking one's enthusiasm. Also when we remain preoccupied with our own little sorrows, they appear big, but when we see others' sorrows, we get the

[1] sahanaṁ sarva-duḥkhānām apratīkāra-pūrvakam,
cintā-vilāpa-rahitaṁ sā titikṣā nigadyate – *Vivekacuḍāmaṇi*-24

strength to bear our own. 'I cried that I did not have shoes, till I saw a child who did not have legs'.

Also what comes, must, by its very nature, go. When we try to run away from or push away the unconducive or run after and hold on to the conducive, we intensify our pain and stress.

The habit of complaining and brooding over a non-conducive situation makes it difficult to bear. Our thoughts about the discomforting situations of life are punctuated with 'commas', not 'full stops'. We say, "It is hot, it is hotter than last year, how can one work in this heat ..." But if one says, "It is hot, full stop"; then one puts an end to the thought, as one has accepted the situation. A mind preoccupied with sorrow cannot think about subtle matters. Hence, titikṣā is an important quality, especially for a spiritual seeker.

***

**Faith:**

श्रद्धा कीदृशी? गुरुवेदान्तवाक्यादिषु विश्वासः श्रद्धा ।।

*śraddhā kīdṛśī? guruvedānta-vākyādiṣu viśvāsaḥ śraddhā.*

श्रद्धा – śraddhā; कीदृशी – what; गुरुवेदान्तवाक्यादिषु – in the words of the Guru and Vedānta; विश्वासः – belief; श्रद्धा – faith

What is the nature of śraddhā? Faith in the words of the Guru and Vedānta (scriptures) is śraddhā.

Faith is a very important factor in our lives. None can live without faith. We sleep with the faith that we shall wake up in the morning. We have faith in the doctor that the medicine he prescribes will cure us. We trust the barber that he will not kill us with the sharpened blade that he puts at our throat. We need to trust that our spouse is faithful to us. A doubting Thomas is never happy (na sukhaṁ saṁśayātmanaḥ).

Belief (mānyatā) may be blind if it is not backed by intellectual enquiry or confirmed by self-experience. Our beliefs may change or break. Blind belief can land us into trouble. It can make us fanatic, close-minded or superstitious.

Here, śraddhā is defined as faith in the words of the Guru and Vedānta (the scriptures). It is an intellectual conviction in the nobility and ability of the Guru and the validity of the scriptures that he teaches. "My Guru is a great soul. What he says is right even though I do not experience it now. The Truth is beyond the mind and the senses. The scriptures indicate this Truth. Hence, they are the valid means of Knowledge. The Guru will interpret the scriptures rightly. He knows the best means for my self-unfoldment. He always has my welfare at heart and will never harm me. He loves me selflessly. He himself is Realised and if I follow his teachings, I too, shall reach this state. I have never seen God. I am not sure if He actually exists. If He does exist, is He formless or with form? But if there is God, the Guru is the only one who can guide me to Him." Such thinking is faith.

Faith is always in the unknown. The known requires no faith as it is already known. I need not have faith that I have a nose. I know it. Tagore says, 'Faith is the bird that sings in joy when the dawn is still dark'. Even though the bird has not seen the sun, it believes that it will soon rise.

Similarly only when there is such a conviction can the seeker walk the path with determination and directly experience what he has faith in (śraddhāvān labhate jñānam). Faith enables us to listen to the scriptures with an open, alert mind. It does not stop enquiry. In fact, it encourages the seeker to reflect upon and realise the Truth. It is therefore not blind. It only gets strengthened through enquiry and culminates in knowledge. Without faith, the seeker will not be able to determine the goal or the means to it. He may also doubt his ability to reach the goal. One without faith destroys oneself (saṁśayātmā vinaśyati).

It is most important to have faith in the Guru, as he can instil in us faith in the scriptures, the means, the goal, and even in our own ability to reach it.

***

**Absorbtion of the Mind:**

समाधानं किम्? चित्तैकाग्रता ।।

*samādhānaṁ kim? cittaikāgratā.*

समाधानं – samādhāna; किम् – what; चित्त-एकाग्रता – single pointedness of the mind

What is samādhāna? It is the single pointedness of the mind.

Normally, the mind wanders and our efforts are distracted, especially when we have not determined our goal or have more than one goal in sight. With a single goal, the mind and our efforts become concentrated and we progress faster. If we want to go to Mumbai (mokṣa), we approach a travel agent (Guru) to make enquiries as to the best mode of transport (sādhana), book our ticket, board the vehicle on time and reach the destination. We control other expenses (the sense organs and the mind), so as to afford the ticket, cancel other programmes that clash with the journey (focus our energies – ekāgratā), have faith in the travel agent and the vehicle that transports us (śraddhā) and endure all the travails of the journey (titikṣā) in order to reach our destination (mokṣa).

Samādhāna is the state of mind when we have a single goal in sight. To reach this goal, one controls the mind (śama) and the senses (dama), withdraws from worldly pursuits (uparama), endures the pinpricks of life (titikṣā) and faithfully follows the path indicated by the Guru and the scriptures (śraddhā). The resultant absorption of the mind in the Self is samādhāna.

***

**Desire for Liberation :**

मुमुक्षुत्वं किम्? मोक्षो मे भूयात् इति इच्छा ।।

*mumukṣutvaṁ kim? mokṣo me bhūyāt iti icchā.*

मुमुक्षुत्वं – mumukṣutva; किम् – what; मोक्षः – Liberation; मे – to me; भूयात् – may it be; इति – thus; इच्छा – desire

What is mumukṣutvam? 'Let me attain Liberation.' This intense desire is mumukṣutvam.

Prompted by the desire for happiness, man runs after objects, people and experiences of the world. He gathers money, attains fame, status and power, travels, enjoys, marries, begets children, and so on. In the process, he experiences various measures of sorrows. At some point in life, he feels, 'Enough is enough. I want to get out of this mess. I shall no more remain a slave to the world and my mind. I refuse to get tossed around by the world. I want to end, not just particular sorrows, but all sorrows for all times to come. I want to free myself from all limitations, feelings of incompleteness, hopelessness and helplessness. I seek that which is permanent and complete'. This desire is called mumukṣutvam.

Most of us do not even know that we are bound. We complacently accept our state of sorrow and finitude as natural. We even try to philosophise about it by saying, "In life sometimes there is brightness and sometimes darkness" – (kabhī dhūp, kabhī chām̐va). Lokmanya Tilak, the great Indian freedom fighter, first had to make the Indians aware that they were not free and that they could be free from foreign rule and govern themselves. Only then would they think about how to go about it. Due to the grace of the Lord, merits of previous births, a shock in one's life or intelligent living and an alert enquiring mind, one starts questioning one's present state of bondage and then desires freedom from it.

Mumukṣutvam is of four types:

a) Very dull (ati manda): "If I get liberated, well and good, otherwise better luck next life". This type cannot be said to possess true mumukṣutvam.

b) Dull (manda): "I must seek Liberation or Truth after I retire or after all my worldly responsibilities are over".

c) Mediocre (madhyama): "I must get liberated as soon as possible. The sooner, the better".

d) Strong (tīvra): "I want freedom from bondage here and now". The intensity of such a desire is like that of the man who seeks air when he is drowning or seeks water when his clothes are on fire. One with strong mumukṣutvam reaches the goal. All other qualities also easily accrue to him.

***

The topic of the fourfold qualification concludes with –

एतत् साधनचतुष्टयम् ।
ततस्तत्त्वविवेकस्याधिकारिणो भवन्ति ।।

*etat sādhana-catuṣṭayam,*
*tatas-tattvavivekasyādhikāriṇo bhavanti.*

एतत् – this; साधनचतुष्टयम् – fourfold qualification; ततः – thereafter; तत्त्वविवेकस्य – of enquiry into the Truth; अधिकारिणः – fit; भवन्ति – become

This is the fourfold qualification. Thereafter, they become fit for the enquiry into the Truth.

When one wants to shoot a target, one begins by preparing the rifle. It is cleaned, oiled and tested to see if its different parts work smoothly and then it is loaded with bullets. Thereafter, one shifts one's attention to the target. Similarly, till such time that the mind is prepared with the fourfold qualification, it is not fit to enquire into the Truth. A prepared mind enquires naturally and spontaneously.

The mind that is forced into thinking will not enquire wholeheartedly, and therefore, not reach the Truth. If the mind is unprepared, then even if one listens to spiritual knowledge, it may seem theoretical and abstract. Even if one appreciates it, one will not be able to reflect on it or abide in it.

## Enquiry into the Truth

What is enquiry into the Truth?

तत्त्वविवेक: क:? आत्मा सत्यं तदन्यत् सर्वं मिथ्येति ।।

*tattvavivekaḥ kaḥ? ātmā satyaṁ tadanyat sarvaṁ mithyeti.*

तत्त्वविवेक: – enquiry into the Truth; क: – what; आत्मा – Self; सत्यम् – Real; तदन्यत् – other than That; सर्वं – all; मिथ्या – is unreal; इति – thus

What is enquiry into the Truth? It is the firm conviction that the Self is real and all, other than That, is unreal.

The discrimination and the determination of what is Real (Self) and what is unreal (the not-Self) constitutes the enquiry into the Truth.

**The discrimination of the Real and unreal:** The Real (Sat) is that which remains the same in all the three periods of time. It does not get negated under any condition and from any standpoint. It is changeless, ever the same. If a person's words stand un-negated through time, we say that he speaks the truth. If he changes his statement now and then, we say, that he utters untruth.

Non-existence (asat) is that which does not exist in all the three periods of time. A barren woman exists and so does a child, but a barren woman's own child (not adopted) can never be.

Unreal (mithyā) is that which cannot be defined as real or non-existent. If a thing exists and is experienced, but keeps changing, it is called unreal. The world exists and is experienced, but it gets negated by time and experience and is hence unreal. Also, what we experience is not what it actually 'is'. Śrī Buddha realised in meditation that this solid looking body is only energy in motion, as is every object of the world. For him it was not just as an intellectual concept as viewed by the scientist, but an actual experience.

**Discrimination of the Self and the not-Self:** There are two aspects to life. 'I' (the experiencer of the world), and the world (the experienced). The name, the form, the quality and the experience of every object of the world changes, but 'I', the experiencer, remains the same. I am never absent, but the world gets negated with every thought. Therefore, 'I' alone am real and all else other than me is unreal.

But right now I understand myself to be the body which is ever-changing. I identify with the mind, but that too is changing and deceptive. Then what is the Self which is supposed to be real and unchanging? The method adopted by the Masters to know the Self is called negating the superimposition (adhyāropa-apavāda). When the not-Self is negated in its entirety, what remains is the pure Self, the Truth.

***

The Self is first defined in negative terms, and then its true nature is asserted.

आत्मा कः?
स्थूलसूक्ष्मकारणशरीराद्-व्यतिरिक्तः पञ्चकोशातीतः सन्
अवस्थात्रय-साक्षी सच्चिदानन्द-स्वरुपः सन् यस्तिष्ठति स आत्मा।।

*ātmā kaḥ?*
*sthūlasūkṣmakāraṇa-śarīrād-vyatiriktaḥ pañcakośātītaḥ san avasthātraya-sākṣī saccidānanda-svarūpaḥ san yastiṣṭhati sa ātmā.*

आत्मा – Self; कः – what – स्थूलसूक्ष्मकारणशरीराद्-व्यतिरिक्तः – other than the gross, subtle and causal bodies; पञ्चकोशातीतः सन् – being beyond the five sheaths; अवस्थात्रय-साक्षी – the witness of the three states of consciousness; सच्चिदानन्द-स्वरुपः सन् – being of the nature of Existence-Consciousness-Bliss; यः – which; तिष्ठति – remains; सः – that; आत्मा – Self

What is the Self? That which is other than the gross, subtle and causal bodies, beyond the five sheaths, the witness of the three states of consciousness and of the nature of Existence-Consciousness-Bliss is the Self.

When asked to introduce ourselves, we talk at length, "I am the son of so and so, my name is 'X', I am a Brāhmaṇa, born in India, in a Hindu family, graduated as an engineer, working in a multinational firm as an executive, earning a five figure salary, 5′ 10″ tall, weighing 75 kgs, fair complexioned, fairly intelligent but bad-tempered and so on. If we analyse closely, we shall understand that we have talked about ourselves only with reference to something else. With respect to my body, 'I' am 5' 10" and 75 kgs. In relation to my father, 'I' am his son, with respect to the firm 'I' am an executive, with respect to my mind 'I' am bad-tempered, with respect to my intellect 'I' am fairly intelligent. Free from these conditionings, what am I or who am I? The conditioning (upādhi) is that which superimposes its quality on that which remains in its proximity. The colourless crystal appears blue or red when kept near a blue or red colour cloth. When the cloth is removed, the crystal is experienced 'as it is', colourless. The three bodies, five sheaths and the three states of consciousness are conditionings of the Self. 'I' the knower of the conditionings am different from the conditionings.

**The three bodies (śarīra-traya):** Each one of us has not one, but three bodies. The gross body (sthūla śarīra) is the one perceived by us through our senses. It is nourished to its present size by food. The subtle body (sūkṣma śarīra) cannot be perceived by the senses, but is known to each one of us. I know when I am hungry. Others may not know of it till I tell them or show signs of it at the physical level. The causal body (kāraṇa śarīra) is the seat of all our inherent tendencies (vāsanās) which are the cause of the other two bodies.

**The five sheaths (pañcakośa):** A man wears layers of clothes when he is out in the snow, but removes them when he comes into his centrally heated home. He is different from the clothes and can put on or remove them at will. Similarly, the Self has covered itself with five sheaths which are nothing but the three bodies (spoken of above), categorised differently. The food sheath (annamaya kośa) is the gross body made up of food. The vital air sheath (prāṇamaya kośa) guides all our physiological activities. The mental sheath (manomaya kośa) is the seat of all emotions. The intellectual sheath (vijñānamaya kośa) guides the body's activities through the notion of doership. The bliss sheath (ānandamaya kośa) also called kāraṇa śarīra, is our personality in its unmanifest condition. The vital air sheath, mental sheath and intellectual sheath together form the subtle body. I know the different conditions of my bodies and sheaths and am therefore different from them.

**The three states of consciousness (avasthātraya):** The three states of consciousness is the total range of experiences that an individual goes through. In the waking state (jāgrat avasthā), we experience the gross world through our senses. In the dream-state (svapna avasthā), we experience our individual dreamworld through our mind. In the deep sleep state (suṣupti avasthā), we experience the absence of the world of objects, emotions or thoughts. I am the witness of all these states. They get mutually negated, but I remain in and through all of them.

**Existence-Consciousness-Bliss (Saccidānanda):** On negating the not-Self, what remains is the pure Self of the nature of Existence-Consciousness-Bliss (saccidānanda svarūpa). Existence (Sat) is that which cannot be negated under any condition. Who can negate the negator? Therefore, I ever exist. Consciousness (Cit) is the Knowledge Principle that illumines all conditionings. Bliss (Ānanda) is more easily understandable than the other two. Conditionings are limitations of time, space and objects. The Self being free from all conditionings is Infinite, and infinity is Bliss.

Knowing my true nature, I get liberated from the limitations of all conditionings. Should we then, not strive for Self-knowledge?

Śrī Śaṅkarācārya now leads us into a more elaborate description of the above definition.

# The Three Bodies

## 1. The Gross Body:

स्थूलशरीरं किम्?
पञ्चीकृतपञ्चमहाभूतैः कृतं सत्कर्मजन्यं
सुखदुःखादिभोगायतनं शरीरम्
अस्ति जायते वर्धते विपरिणमते अपक्षीयते विनश्यतीति
षड्विकारवदेतत् स्थूलशरीरम्।।

*sthūlaśarīraṁ kim?*
*pañcīkṛta-pañcamahābhūtaiḥ kṛtaṁ satkarmajanyaṁ*
*sukhaduḥkhādi-bhogāyatanaṁ śarīram*
*asti jāyate vardhate vipariṇamate apakṣīyate vinaśyatīti*
*ṣadvikāravad-etat sthūlaśarīram.*

स्थूलशरीरं – gross body; किम् – what; पञ्चीकृत-पञ्चमहाभूतैः – by the five great elements that have undergone the process of pañcīkaraṇa; कृतं – made; सत्कर्मजन्यं – born of the result of good actions of the past; सुखदुःखादि-भोगायतनं – a counter for the experience of joy, sorrow etc; शरीरम् – body; अस्ति – is; जायते – is born; वर्धते – grows; विपरिणमते – matures; अपक्षीयते – decays; विनश्यतीति – and dies; षड्विकारवत् – with six modifications; एतत् – this; स्थूलशरीरम् – gross body

That which is made up of the five great elements that have undergone the process of pañcīkaraṇa, born as a result of the good actions of the past, the counter of experiences like joy, sorrow and so on and subject to the six modifications namely – to exist, to be born, to grow, to mature, to decay and to die – is the gross body.

Presently, our mind is focussed on the gross plane and so let us start the analysis with the gross body.

**Made up of the five great elements which have undergone the process of grossification:** The five great elements are space, air, fire, water and earth. When they undergo a process of grossification (described later in the text) they form the five gross elements. A permutation and combination of these constitute the entire gross world that we perceive. Our body too, is part of this world and hence, made up of the five gross elements.

**Gross body (sthūla śarīra):** We can perceive our own and other bodies with the five senses. It is therefore called the 'gross body'. It disintegrates with time and is therefore called śarīra (śīryamāṇatvāt śarīram). At death the body disintegrates to merge with the five elements from which it is formed. Death therefore, causes the body to attain to the five elements (pañcatvam āpuḥ). Actually, the body being part of the five elements is never separate from them. None of the five elements separately or together belong to us, yet I regard this body which is a combination of the five elements to be me and things related to this body as mine.

**This (etat):** The body, like every other object, can be indicated as 'this'. 'I' the knower of 'this', am different from it.

**Born as a result of actions (satkarmajanyaṁ):** This body is the result of actions done in the past. The human birth is the best in the entire creation. In this birth, we have the choice to evolve or devolve. We are endowed with a subtle intellect that can discriminate between right and wrong, real and unreal and attain the supreme Truth. Human birth is surely the result of good actions done in the past[1]. Knowing its rarity and uniqueness, we should not waste this precious birth but achieve the purpose for which we gained this body.

**Counter of experiences (sukha-duḥkha-ādi-bhoga-āyatanaṁ):** In a shop, all transactions take place at the counter. When the counter closes, all transactions – the incoming and outgoing – are stopped. Similarly, this body is the counter through which we reap our experiences of joy and sorrow. These transactions temporarily cease when we sleep and permanently, at death. The body is also compared to a city with nine gates (nava dvāra pura). Just as traffic passes through the gates, the transactions of life happen through the nine orifices of the body. For example, we eat through the mouth and so on.

**Six modifications (ṣaḍvikāravat):** The body undergoes six modifications:

---

[1] baḍe bhāga mānuṣa tanu pāvā – *Rāma-carita-mānas, Uttarakāṇḍa*-42.4

1) Existence (asti): The mother experiences changes within and the doctor confirms the 'presence' of the foetus in the mother's womb.

2) Is born (jāyate): After nine months, the child emerges from the mother's womb to experience the outer world.

3) Grows (vardhate): Nourished by food, the body grows.

4) Matures (vipariṇamate): It attains adolescence, matures and in due course of time, attains its peak physical vitality.

5) Decays (apakṣīyate): Then, slowly the limbs weaken, the hair greys, the skin loosens and energy ebbs away.

6) Dies (vinaśyati): Finally it disintegrates to totally merge with its constituent elements. We call this death.

'I', the pure Self, am a witness to all the modifications of the body. 'I' am neither born, nor do 'I' die with the body. Only out of false identification do I say, 'I am dying', 'I am fat' and so on. I need not neglect the body because of knowledge that I am different from the body. It is a vehicle that we use to transact with the world and is meant for performing good actions (śarīram-ādyaṁ khalu dharma-sādhanaṁ). It is the temple which houses the pure Self within (deho devālayaḥ proktaḥ). It should therefore be kept clean and fit for use. We need not get too attached to it or falsely identify with it.

***

**2. The Subtle Body:**

सूक्ष्मशरीरं किम्?
अपञ्चीकृतपञ्चमहाभूतैः कृतं सत्कर्मजन्यं
सुखदुःखादिभोगसाधनं पञ्चज्ञानेन्द्रियाणि पञ्चकर्मेन्द्रियाणि
पञ्चप्राणादयः मनश्चैकं–बुद्धिश्चैका एवं सप्तदशकलाभिः सह
यत्तिष्ठति तत्सूक्ष्मशरीरम्।।

*sūkṣmaśarīraṁ kim?*
*apañcīkṛta-pañcamahābhūtaiḥ kṛtaṁ satkarmajanyaṁ*
*sukhaduḥkhādi-bhoga-sādhanaṁ pañca-jñānendriyāṇi*
*pañca-karmendriyāṇi pañca-prāṇādayaḥ manaścaikaṁ*
*buddhiścaikā evaṁ saptadaśa-kalābhiḥ saha*
*yattiṣṭhati tat-sūkṣma-śarīram.*

सूक्ष्मशरीरं – subtle body; किम् – what; अपञ्चीकृत-पञ्चमहाभूतैः – by the five great elements which have not undergone grossification; कृतं – made; सत्कर्मजन्यं – born of the good actions of the past; सुखदुःखादि-भोगसाधनं – the instrument for the experience of joy, sorrow and so on; पञ्चज्ञानेन्द्रियाणि – the five organs of perception; पञ्चकर्मेन्द्रियाणि – the five organs of actions; पञ्चप्राणादयः – the five prāṇas; मनःच एकम् – a mind; बुद्धिः च एका – an intellect; एवम् – in this way; सप्तदशकलाभिः सह – with seventeen constituents; यत् – which; तिष्ठति – remain; तत् – that; सूक्ष्मशरीरम् – subtle body

What is the subtle body? That which is composed of the five great elements which have not undergone grossification, born of the good actions of the past, the instrument for the experience of joy, sorrow and so on, constituted of seventeen items (the five sense organs, the five organs of action, the five prāṇas, the mind and the intellect) is the subtle body.

Pervading the gross body is the subtle body.

**Made of ungrossified elements (apañcākṛta-pañcamahābhutaiḥ kṛtaṁ):** The five great elements in their nascent form are called tanmātrās. The entire subtle world is constituted from their permutation and combination. The subtle body being a part of the subtle world is also made up of these subtle elements.

They are called subtle, as they cannot be perceived by our senses. I cannot see another's mind (thank God!) nor my own with my gross eyes. But I am aware of the thoughts of my mind (sākṣi-bhāsya). The subtle body enlivens the gross body. When it leaves the gross body we say that the person is dead and gone. It is also called 'liṅga śarīra' as it reveals the presence of life.

**Born of Results of Actions (satkarma-janyaṁ):** As already discussed, the human birth is the result of the good actions of the past. With the prominence of merits, we gain a heavenly body, with demerits, an animal's or lower body and with the balance of both, we gain a human body[1]. In both, the higher and the lower bodies, our merits or demerits are exhausted with no new ones being formed (bhoga-janma). In the human body alone we can harvest a rich crop of merits and demerits

---

[1] puṇyena puṇyaṁ lokaṁ nayati, pāpena pāpam ubhābhyām eva manuṣyalokam. – *Praśnopaniṣad*-3.7

through our actions (karma-janma). Our actions differ, and therefore, our subtle bodies are also different. Even identical twins think differently from each other.

**Instrument of Experiences (bhoga-sādhanaṁ):** It is the mind and intellect or the subtle body that actually experiences joys, sorrows, heat, cold, and so on. The body feels neither pain nor honour when pricked or garlanded. It is the mind that recognises them. The book you hold is unaware that you hold it, as it has no subtle body; but you are aware that you hold it, through the functioning of your subtle body. Therefore, in the deep sleep state, when the mind-intellect stop functioning temporarily, there is no experience of the world.

**The Seventeen Components (saptadaśa-kalāḥ):** The seventeen components of the subtle body are the five sense organs, the five organs of action, the five prāṇas, the mind and the intellect. The capacity to perceive and cognise does not lie in the external organs, but rather in something subtler and beyond them. The external organ (golaka) is a part of the gross body. By itself it cannot perceive or respond to any stimuli. For example, even the blind man has eyes, but no sight. The faculty of sight that lies behind the eye is the actual sense organ.

The prāṇas are the physiological functions without which the body cannot remain alive. They supply energy to the gross and subtle bodies. The mind is the seat of emotions, perceptions and the capacity of volition. The intellect recognises, observes, judges, analyses, conceptualises, imagines and decides. The mind and intellect prompt the body into action. The subtle body is thus, the driver of the body which is like a vehicle. The subtle body is the real cause of all our success and failures in life.

## 2.1 Organs of Perception (jñānendriyāṇi):

श्रोत्रं त्वक् चक्षुः रसना घ्राणं इति पञ्चज्ञानेन्द्रियाणि ।
श्रोत्रस्य दिग्देवता। त्वचो वायुः। चक्षुषः सूर्यः। रसनाया वरुणः।
घ्राणस्य अश्विनौ। इति ज्ञानेन्द्रियदेवताः।
श्रोत्रस्य विषयः शब्दग्रहणम्। त्वचो विषयः स्पर्शग्रहणम्।
चक्षुषो विषयः रूपग्रहणम् । रसनाया विषयः रसग्रहणम् ।
घ्राणस्य विषयः गन्धग्रहणम् इति।।

*śrotraṁ tvak cakṣuḥ rasanā ghrāṇaṁ iti*
*pañcajñānendriyāṇi,*
*śrotrasya digdevatā, tvaco vāyuḥ, cakṣuṣaḥ sūryaḥ,*
*rasanāyā varuṇaḥ, ghrāṇasya aśvinau,*
*iti jñānendriya-devatāḥ,*
*srotrasya viṣayaḥ śabda-grahaṇam, tvaco viṣayaḥ*
*sparśa-grahaṇam,*
*cakṣuṣo viṣayaḥ rūpa-grahaṇam,*
*rasanāyā viṣayaḥ rasa-grahaṇam,*
*ghrāṇasya viṣayaḥ gandha-grahaṇam iti.*

श्रोत्रं – ear; त्वक् – skin; चक्षुः – eye; रसना – tongue; घ्राणं – nose; इति पञ्चज्ञानेन्द्रियाणि – are the five sense organs; श्रोत्रस्य – of the ear; दिग्देवता – Space; त्वचः – of the skin; वायुः – Air; चक्षुषः – of the eye; सूर्यः – Sun; रसनायाः – of the tongue; वरुणः – Water; घ्राणस्य – of the nose; अश्विनौ – the two Aśvini Kumāras; इति

ज्ञानेन्द्रियदेवता: – are the presiding deities of the sense organs; श्रोत्रस्य – of the ear; विषय: – field of experience; शब्दग्रहणम् – receiving sound; त्वच: – of the skin; विषय: – field of experience; स्पर्शग्रहणम् – receiving touch; चक्षुष: – of the eye; विषय: – field of experience; रुपग्रहणम् - cognition of form; रसनाया: – of the tongue; विषय: – field of experience; रसग्रहणम् – cognition of taste; घ्राणस्य – of the nose; विषय: – field of experience; गन्धग्रहणम् – is cognition of smell; इति – thus

The five organs of perception are the ears, skin, eyes, tongue and nose. The presiding deities of the organs of perception are Space of the ears, Air of the skin, the Sun of the eyes, Water of the tongue and the two Aśvini Kumāras of the nose. The fields of experience for the organs of perception are, cognition of sound for the ear; cognition of touch for the skin, cognition of form for the eyes; cognition of taste for the tongue and cognition of smell for the nose.

The five organs of perception have the capacity to hear (located in the ears), feel (located in the skin), see (located in the eyes), taste (located in the tongue) and smell (located in the nose). Through these we perceive the entire world of sound, touch, form, taste and smell, respectively. Each sense organ perceives only its own particular sense objects. There is no admixture of duties. The ears cannot see nor the nose taste. One-fifth of the world of perception is cut-off, if one of them fails to function. For example, there is no perception of form and colour for the visually challenged. When one of the senses is weak or not functioning, the others become sharper. The visually challenged therefore, have keen ears. Knowledge gained through the senses is called direct perception (pratyakṣa jñānam). Most of our knowledge is by direct perception or based on it. Based on what we perceive, we respond. If the perception is faulty, our response will be improper. A deaf person cannot easily articulate words, as he has never heard sounds. Hence, the senses play a very important role in our lives.

Every department in an organisation has a departmental head who is responsible for managing and controlling the functioning of that department. Even an automatic machine needs a person to maintain it regularly, to switch it on or off, and to repair it when in need. Hence without a sentient entity, the inert cannot function. In the Hindu scriptures, these sentient beings that control the functioning of the various functions of the universe are said to be thirty-three crores in number and are called devatās or presiding deities. It is to be clearly understood that Hindus believe in one God (Īśvara) alone, but they accept that every functional head draws his power, strength and knowledge from the one omnipotent God. Dig-devatā heads the faculty of hearing as sound travels in the medium of space. Vāyu, the air controls touch. Sūrya or Sun is the source of all light on the earth and seeing is possible only in the presence of light, hence the Sun is the deity of sight. A dry tongue has no taste. When we hear of something tasty, our mouth waters. Varuṇa or Water is the deity of taste. The two Aśvini Kumāras guide the functioning of smell.

The conditions of the senses are known to me, hence I am different from them and the objects they perceive.

**Organs of Perception**

| Name of the organ | Ability to hear in the ears | Ability to feel in the skin | Ability to see in the eyes | Ability to taste in the tongue | Ability to smell in the nose |
|---|---|---|---|---|---|
| Presiding Deity | Dig Devatā | Vāyu | Sūrya | Varuṇa | Aśvini Kumāras |
| Function | Hearing | Feeling | Seeing | Tasting | Smelling |
| Sense objects perceived | Sound | Touch | Form and Colour | Taste | Smell |

## 2.2 Organs of Action (karmendriyāṇi)

वाक्पाणिपादपायूपस्थानीति पञ्चकर्मेन्द्रियाणि ।
वाचो देवता वह्निः। हस्तयोरिन्द्रः। पादयोर्विष्णुः।
पायोर्मृत्युः। उपस्थस्य प्रजापतिः। इति कर्मेन्द्रियदेवताः।
वाचो विषयः भाषणम्। पाण्योर्विषयः वस्तुग्रहणम्।
पादयोर्विषयः गमनम् । पायोर्विषयः मलत्यागः।
उपस्थस्य विषयः आनन्द इति।।

*vākpāṇipāda-pāyūpasthānīti pañca-karmendriyāṇi,*
*vāco devatā vahniḥ, hastayor-indraḥ, pādayor-viṣṇuḥ,*
*pāyor-mṛtyuḥ, upasthasya prajāpatiḥ,*
*iti karmendriya-devatāḥ, vāco viṣayaḥ bhāṣaṇam,*
*pāṇyor-viṣayaḥ vastugrahaṇam, pādayor-viṣayaḥ*
*gamanam, pāyor-viṣayaḥ malatyāgaḥ,*
*upasthasya viṣayaḥ ānanda iti.*

वाक्-पाणि-पाद-पायू-उपस्थानि-इति – speech, hands, legs, the anus, the genitals; पञ्चकर्मेन्द्रियाणि – are the five organs of action;

वाचः – of speech; देवता – deity; वह्निः – Fire; हस्तयोः – of the hands; इन्द्रः – Indra; पादयोः – of the legs; विष्णुः – Viṣṇu; पायोः – of the anus; मृत्युः – Death; उपस्थस्य – of the genitals; प्रजापतिः – Prajāpati; इति कर्मेन्द्रियदेवताः – these are the presiding deities of the organs of action; वाचः विषयः – the function of speech; भाषणम् – to speak; पाण्योः विषयः – the function of the hands; वस्तुग्रहणम – to grasp things; पादयोः विषयः – the function of the legs; गमनम् – locomotion; पायोः विषयः – the function of the anus; मलत्याग : – eliminate waste; उपस्थस्य विषयः – the function of the genitals; आनन्दः इति – is pleasure

The five organs of action are: speech, hands, legs, anus and the genitals. The presiding deities of the organs of action are: Agni (Fire) of speech, Indra of the hands, Viṣṇu of the legs, Yama of the anus and Prajāpati of the genitals. The function of speech is to speak, that of the hands is to grasp things, of the legs is locomotion, of the anus is the elimination of waste and of the genitals is pleasure (procreation).

The five organs of action are the capacity to speak (located in the vocal chords and tongue), to grasp things (located in the hands), of locomotion (located in the legs), to excrete (located in the anus) and to procreate (located in the genitals). The body responds to external stimuli through them. They are prompted by the mind into action. They develop from childhood, attain their full strength and then weaken with age. Each of them carries out its respective function. In rare cases the other organs of action try to do the function of the impaired organ. For example, some learn to write with the toes of the feet when the hands are amputed.

The tongue has a unique place, as it is both an organ of action (eating and speaking) and of perception (tasting).

Fire is the deity of speech which is well understood by expressions such as 'fiery speech,' or 'heated discussion'. Heat is generated when one speaks. Indra, the king of the deities is responsible for the functioning of the hands. The forelegs of animals have evolved to become our hands. All art is possible due to the unique capacity of our fingers. Viṣṇu, the one with long strides, is the deity of the legs. Mṛtyu (Death) presides over the anus. Man is known to eliminate waste from the various orifices at death. Prajāpati, the Creator, is in charge of procreation. The pleasure in the act of reproduction ensures the continuity of the species.

**The Organs of Action**

| **Name of the organ** | **Capacity to speak located in tongue** | **Ability to grasp in hands** | **Locomotion in legs** | **Ability to excrete in anus** | **Capacity to procreate in genitals** |
|---|---|---|---|---|---|
| Presiding Deity | Agni | Indra | Viṣṇu | Mṛtyu | Prajāpati |
| Function | Speech | Grasping | Locomotion | Elimination of waste | Procreation |

***

**3 Causal Body:**

कारणशरीरं किम्?
अनिर्वाच्यानाद्यविद्यारूपं शरीरद्वयस्य कारणमात्रं सत्स्वरूपाज्ञानं।
निर्विकल्पकरूपं यदस्ति तत्कारणशरीरम्।।

*kāraṇa śarīaṁ kim?*
*anirvācyānādyavidyārūpaṁ*
*śarīra-dvayasya kāraṇa-mātraṁ satsvarūpājñānaṁ,*
*nirvikalpaka-rūpaṁ yadasti tat-kāraṇa-śarīram.*

कारणशरीरं – causal body; किम् – what; अनिर्वाच्य – inexplicable; अनादि – beginningless; अविद्यारूपं – in the form of ignorance; शरीरद्वयस्य – of the two bodies; कारणमात्रं – the sole cause; सत्-स्वरूप-अज्ञानं – ignorance of one's own true nature; निर्विकल्पकरूपं – free from duality; यत् – which; अस्ति – is; तत् – that; कारणशरीरम् – causal body

That which is inexplicable, beginningless, in the form of ignorance, the sole cause of the two bodies (gross and subtle), ignorance of one's own true nature, free from duality, is the causal body.

The causal body is the subtlest of the three bodies and pervades the other two.

**avidyā-rūpaṁ:** It is of the nature of ignorance. Ignorance has no shape, size or quality. It is always related to an object. For example, ignorance of computers. But by itself, it is objectless. 'I' am the locus of ignorance. Ignorance cannot exist without me. I exist, therefore, I can be ignorant.

**anirvācya:** Ignorance is inexplicable.

a) Since it has no shape, size or quality, it cannot be described by words or grasped by the mind.

b) Ignorance implies lack of knowledge. It does not actually have any existence. Yet it cannot be said to be non-existent. We experience its effects. It manifests as the gross and the subtle bodies and we also experience sorrow caused by ignorance.

c) Being nothing, it still does a great deal, hence it is an inexplicable power.

**anādi:** Ignorance is beginningless. If we say that ignorance began at a particular time, then there should have been either a void or knowledge before that. But ignorance cannot emerge from nothing or from knowledge. Therefore neither void nor knowledge can precede ignorance. Therefore ignorance is beginningless.

**śarīra dvayasya kāraṇa mātraṁ:** Ignorance is the cause of the two bodies. I mistake a rope for a snake. I feel scared and run away from it. Ignorance of the rope caused the notion of the snake which gave rise to fear in the mind, which in turn prompted the body to run. Similarly, not knowing my true nature, I mistakenly identify with the finite, feel a sense of incompleteness, desire to fulfil myself, so run after objects thinking that they would make me happy. Ignorance is at the root of all my actions. Actions give results which I enjoy or suffer and that leave behind tendencies (vāsanās) which prompt future desires-actions-results. Hence, we can also say that inherent tendencies prompt actions. We have already seen that the two bodies, gross and subtle, are the result of inherent tendencies otherwise called the causal body.

**sat-svarūpa-ajñānaṁ:** Ignorance of our true nature. I know I exist. I do not however, know that my own true nature is Existence-Consciousness-Bliss. I think I am the body, the doer of actions and enjoyer of results. It is strange that I know so much about the world, but do not know the 'knower' of the world at all. And it is all the more ironic, that the knower is me alone! I do not know who I really am.

**nirvikalpakarūpaṁ:** Ignorance is homogenous. It has no difference. It has no dualities of the knower and the known. Ignorance cannot be known. Knowledge dispels it. My ignorance cannot be different from yours. The object of ignorance may differ but ignorance remains the same. There are degrees in knowledge, but not in ignorance. Being beyond thought (vikalpa), it is without thoughts (nirvikalpa).

Ignorance can be destroyed by knowledge. Therefore, the causal body is not eternal. The Self, being beyond birth and death, is eternal. Hence I am different from the causal body. Thus, knowing my true nature, I experience myself as different from all the three bodies – gross, subtle and causal.

# The Three States

अवस्थात्रयं किम् ? जाग्रत्स्वप्नसुषुप्त्यवस्था:।।

*avasthātrayaṁ kim? jāgratsvapna-suṣuptyavasthāḥ.*

अवस्थात्रयं – three states; किम् – what; जाग्रत्–स्वप्न–सुषुप्ति–अवस्था: – the waking, dream and deep sleep states

What are the three states? They are the waking, dream and deep sleep states.

The range of human experience is wide and varied. I experience the physical world as sound, touch, form, taste and smell; the emotional world as desire, anger, love and compassion and the intellectual world as ideals, concepts, imagination and so on. I also experience the absence of all of them. These experiences are divided into the three states of consciousness which we all go through, each day of our lives. They are the waking, dream and deep sleep states.

***

**The Waking State:**

जाग्रदवस्था का?
श्रोत्रादिज्ञानेन्द्रियै: शब्दादिविषयैश्च
ज्ञायते इति या सा जाग्रदवस्था ।
स्थूलशरीराभिमानी आत्मा विश्व इत्युच्यते।।

*jāgradavasthā kā? śrotrādi-jñānendriyaiḥ śabdādi viṣayaiśca jñāyate iti yā sā jāgrad-avasthā, sthula-śarīrābhimānī ātmā viśva ityucyate.*

जाग्रदवस्था – the waking state; का – what; श्रोत्रादि-ज्ञानेन्द्रियै: – with the organs of perception like the ears etc.; शब्दादि-विषयै: च – the sense objects like sound etc.; ज्ञायते – are perceived; इति – thus; या – that; जाग्रदवस्था – waking state; स्थूलशरीर-अभिमानी – identified with the gross body; आत्मा – the Self; विश्व – Viśva; इति उच्यते – is called

What is the waking state? That state of experience in which the sense objects like sound are perceived through the sense organs like the ears, is the waking state. The Self, identifying with the gross body, is then called 'Viśva'.

Waking is the state of experience where my entire personality is awake and fully functioning. I identify with all the three bodies and experience the world through them. The waker is therefore, called Viśva – complete or all-inclusive.

I am identified with the gross body only in the waking state and not in the dream or deep sleep state, and therefore, it is mentioned that in the waking state I identify with the gross body. It is not possible to function through the gross body without identifying with the subtle and causal bodies. I cannot read or hold this book without my mind backing my eyes and hands.

Since the gross body, which is the counter of experience is open, all transactions happen through it. The objects in the waking world are experienced through the sense organs as being outside the body. The book that you hold does not seem to be within you, but outside you. I act with the notion of doership (kartṛtvam) and thereby, also enjoy the results (bhoktṛtvam).

The waking world seems to be solid and real. Objects and events seem to have a cause-effect relationship. They have their uses and functions according to some laws. I wake up each day to the same familiar world. I therefore, give the waking state a greater reality and importance. I form attachments to objects and beings and enjoy or suffer them. However, I dismiss my dreams as unreal because I see them as a figment of my imagination.

***

**The Dream State:**

स्वप्नावस्था केति चेत् । जाग्रदवस्थायां यद्
दृष्टं यत् श्रुतं तज्जनितवासनया निद्रासमये यः
प्रपञ्चः प्रतीयते सा स्वप्नावस्था।
सूक्ष्मशरीराभिमानी आत्मा तैजस इत्युच्यते।।

*svapnāvasthā keti cet, jāgradavasthāyāṁ yad*
*dṛṣṭaṁ yat śrutaṁ tajjanita-vāsanayā nīdrā-samaye yaḥ*
*prapañcaḥ pratīyate sā svapnāvasthā,*
*sūkṣmaśarīrābhimānī ātmā taijasa ityucyate.*

स्वप्नावस्था – the dream state; का इति चेत् – if asked what it is; जाग्रदवस्थायाम् – in the waking state; यद् – which; दृष्टं –

seen; यद् – which; श्रुतं – heard; तत्-जनित-वासनया – by the impressions born from that; निद्रासमये – at the time of sleep; यः – which; प्रपञ्चः – world; प्रतीयते – experienced; सा – that; स्वप्न-अवस्था – dream state; सूक्ष्मशरीर-अभिमानी – identified with the subtle body; आत्मा – the Self; तैजसः – Taijasa; इति उच्यते – is called

For the question, 'What is the dream state?', the explanation is: The world that is projected while in sleep from the impressions born of what was seen and heard in the waking state, is called the dream state. The Self identified with the subtle body is called Taijasa.

Seeing is believing. Also, most of our knowledge in the waking world is gathered through hearing. Therefore, the eyes and the ears are the main sources of gaining experiences. Experiences gained through them, the other senses, the mind and the intellect in the waking state form impressions in the mind. The more intense or more repetitive the experience, the deeper are the impressions.

The mind creates, sustains and ends the dreamworld. Not only the world, but also the enjoyer of this world (the dreamer) is created by the mind. The dreamer can have an entirely different identity from the waker. The conscious thinking by the intellect has no role to play in the dream state. Also, there is no notion of doership and hence no merit or demerit is created in the dream. There is only the notion of enjoyership (bhoktṛtvam), but again there is no choice about whether to enjoy or to suffer.

Dreams are the unfulfilled wishes of the waker or the garbled impressions of the waking state, that do not require gross manifestation. One may dream of winning a lottery ticket or of a horse flying. The dream may seem strange or the sights illogical or ridiculous to the waker, but the dreamer does not feel so. The Self does not identify with the gross body then, but only with the subtle and causal bodies. The individual is then called Taijasa, as the dreamworld is thought-created (tejomaya antaḥkaraṇa-vṛtti-rūpatvāt taijasaḥ). The dream may seem unreal to the waker, but it is very real to the dreamer.

***

**The Deep Sleep State:**

अथ सुषुप्त्यवस्था का?
अहं किमपि न जानामि
सुखेन मया निद्राऽनुभूयत इति सुषुप्त्यवस्था।
कारणशरीराभिमानी आत्मा प्राज्ञ इत्युच्यते।।

*atha suṣuptyavasthā kā?*
*ahaṁ kimapi na jānāmi*
*sukhena mayā nidrā'nubhūyata iti suṣuptyavasthā,*
*kāraṇa-śarīrābhimānī ātmā prājña ityucyate.*

अथ – then; सुषुप्त्यवस्था – deep sleep state; का – what; अहम् – I; किमपि – anything; न जानामि – do not know; सुखेन – happily; मया – by me; निद्रा – sleep; अनुभूयते – experienced; इति सुषुप्त्यवस्था – is the deep sleep state; कारणशरीर-अभिमानी –

identified with the causal body; आत्मा – Self; प्राज्ञ: – Prājña; इति उच्यते – is called

Then what is the deep sleep state? That state about which one says, "I did not know anything, I enjoyed good sleep", is the deep sleep state. The Self identified with the causal body is called Prājña.

When one gives up identification with the gross and subtle bodies and identifies only with the causal body, one is said to be in the deep sleep state. In that state, one experiences the absence of all objects, emotions and thoughts. When one awakens from it one says, "I did not know anything but I was happy. I slept well". This memory of having slept well or otherwise, proves the presence of 'I', the experiencer, even in the absence of the world. Hence the joy experienced is of one's own true nature. Due to ignorance we do not know this and so we wake up as ignorant as ever, looking for joy in the world of objects yet again.

In the waking state I identify with the gross body and become the doer and enjoyer. In the dream state I identify with the subtle body and become the enjoyer of the dreamworld. In the deep sleep state there is neither the doer of actions nor the enjoyer of the world. In the absence of thoughts, there is no concept of time, space or duality. Hence I cannot say how long I slept or where I was in sleep.

In the waking and dream states I know I exist, but I do not know my true nature. I take myself to be the gross and subtle bodies and accept the waking and the dreamworlds to be real. In the deep sleep state, I am ignorant of my true nature and also of the world. Except for the awareness that 'I exist', there is total ignorance, and therefore, the individual is called Prājña (prāyeṇa ajñaḥ – one who is more or less ignorant).

The waking and dream state of each of us differs but the deep sleep state is the same for all. The king, the beggar, the ignorant one and the wise man – all experience bliss in the deep sleep state. There are no degrees in this bliss. It is homogeneous, partless and complete. Therefore, we do not want to come out of it. We are refreshed and rejuvenated by this state. If we are sleepless for even a day, we become distraught. We willingly give up the whole world to go to sleep. Some even take sleeping tablets to induce this state. We go to this state either from the waking or the dream state, when tired physically or mentally and being overpowered by inertia. The unmanifest impressions (vāsanās) of the waking world manifest to push us out of this state either into the dream or the waking world. There are also some 'in-between' states that we experience. The sleep walker is both awake and asleep. One in a half sleep state is neither awake nor asleep. The day dreamer is both aware and dreaming.

The three states come and go. Each negates the experience and reality of the other two. I am the witness of these states. I stand un-negated by them. I may act like a beggar in a play, but I do not become a beggar. Similarly, I am not the roles I take up of the waker, dreamer, or deep sleeper.

# The Five Sheaths

पञ्चकोशा: के ?
अन्नमय: प्राणमय: मनोमय: विज्ञानमय: आनन्दमयश्चेति।।

*pañcakośāḥ ke? annamayaḥ prāṇamayaḥ manomayaḥ vijñānamayaḥ ānandamayaśceti.*

पञ्चकोशा: – the five sheaths; के– what; अन्नमय: – food sheath प्राणमय: – vital air sheath; मनोमय: – mental sheath; विज्ञानमय: – intellectual sheath; आनन्दमय: – bliss sheath; च – and; इति – thus

What are the five sheaths? They are the food sheath, vital air sheath, mental sheath, intellectual sheath and the bliss sheath.

Kośa means a covering (kośavat ācchādayati tasmāt kośaḥ). The scabbard of the sword covers the sword. It is of the same shape as the sword. It indicates the presence of the sword even though it covers the sword from one's sight. The scabbard is always different from the sword and does not affect the sword in any way. Similarly, the Self is covered by five sheaths. The fact that I see, think, feel and so on, indicates the presence of 'I'. The functioning of these sheaths proves the presence of the Self. But they cover the true nature of the Self. The five sheaths are of my making, but I get so identified with them that I am bound by them and am unable to free myself. Even though I am essentially always free from them, I get attached and affected by them, and therefore, suffer. We have to discover the Self as beyond the five sheaths.

***

**The Food Sheath:**

अन्नमय: क:?
अन्नरसेनैव भूत्वा अन्नरसेनैव वृद्धिं प्राप्य अन्नरूपपृथिव्यां
यद्विलीयते तदन्नमय: कोश: स्थूलशरीरम्।।

*annamayaḥ kaḥ?*
*annarasenaiva bhūtvā annarasenaiva*
*vṛddhiṁ prāpya annarūpa-pṛthivyāṁ yadvilīyate*
*tadannamayaḥ kośaḥ sthūla-śarīram.*

अन्नमय: – annamaya; क: – what; अन्नरसेन एव – by the essence of food alone; भूत्वा – having been born; अन्नरसेन एव – by the essence of food alone; वृद्धिं – growth; प्राप्य – having attained; अन्न-रूप-पृथिव्यां – into the earth which is of the nature of food; यद् – which; विलीयते – merges; तत् – that; अन्नमय: कोश: – the food sheath; स्थूलशरीरम् – gross body

What is the food sheath? That which is born from the essence of food, grows by the essence of food and merges into the earth, which is the nature of food is called the food sheath or the gross body.

The word 'maya' in annamaya means modifications. The body is the result of modification of food and hence called annamaya. The food eaten is digested. Its very essence becomes the sperm in man and the ovum in woman. They combine to form the seed from which the foetus is formed. It is nourished in the womb by the food eaten by the mother. At birth the child emerges from the womb and is nourished by the mother's milk. It grows up and develops in strength and size due to the food eaten. We consume mountains of food in our lifetime. Finally we die to merge into food (earth). The earth itself becomes the food we eat, and therefore, from earth we are born to go back to the earth, or one can say that we are born from food and go back to food.

Food is that which is eaten by beings and which eats beings[1]. We eat food and food in turn eats us. Many die by overeating. Also the body gets eaten by many viruses and bacteria even while we are alive, and by worms and other beings when we die. The soil from which we are shaped in turn gets converted into food eaten by others. Identifying with the annamaya kośa, I say, 'I am tall, fair' and so on.

***

**The Vital Air Sheath:**

प्राणमय: क:?
प्राणाद्या: पञ्चवायव: वागादीन्द्रियपञ्चकं प्राणमय: कोश:।।

*prāṇamayaḥ kaḥ?*
*prāṇādyāḥ pañcavāyavaḥ vāgādīndriya-pañcakaṁ prāṇamayaḥ kośaḥ.*

1 adyate'tti ca bhūtāni, tasmāt-annaṁ taducyata iti.
– *Taittirīya Upaniṣad*-II.ii.1

प्राणमय: – vital air (sheath); क: – what; प्राणाद्या: – prāṇa etc.; पञ्चवायव: – five air modifications; वागादि-इन्द्रियपञ्चक – the five organs of action like speech etc.; प्राणमय: कोश: – vital air sheath

What is vital air sheath? The five physiological functions like prāṇa and so on, and the five organs of action like speech and so on, together form the vital air sheath.

The vital air sheath pervades the food sheath. It is subtler than the food sheath. The five modifications of air (vāyu-vikāra) which control the main physiological functions of the body are called prāṇas. They are:

1. Prāṇa: Breathing is governed by the prāṇa. When the inhalation and exhalation is slow, deep, rhythmic and even, then the breathing is proper and good.

2. Apāna: The evacuation and rejection of all waste from the body is taken care of by apāna. Were it not for its efficient functioning, toxic chemicals and waste would gather in the body.

3. Vyāna: The circulation of blood and nourishment to every cell of the body is the work of vyāna. When one sits in a particular posture for a long time and the blood does not circulate freely, one commonly experiences leg cramps and the like.

4. Udāna: All reactions or reverse processes are done by udāna. For example, vomiting, burping, shedding tears and sneezing. It is responsible for the continous and emerging thoughts of the mind. It supplies the

necessary power to the subtle body to leave the gross body at death.

5. Samāna: The food eaten is digested and assimilated by samāna.

The five prāṇas are vital to life. They function silently from birth to death even while we sleep. If even one of them were to stop completely, we would die. They connect the subtle body to the gross body and energise both. When they function efficiently, the body remains healthy, the sense organs are keen, the organs of action strong and the mind alert. When they malfunction, the body becomes ill, imbalanced, weak, dull and diseased. Hence the emphasis on prāṇāyāma – control of the prāṇas – in the Yoga-śāstras. We can control the prāṇas through the mind. Yogīs are known to be able to stop their breathing or heart beat and breathe from their rib bone and so on. Normally, they function naturally and involuntarily. Fortunately, one does not have to learn how to breathe or digest. They are inherent and they keep happening unconsciously.

The five prāṇas and the organs of action together are called the prāṇamaya kośa. Identified with it, man says, 'I am hungry, thirsty' and so on.

***

**The Mental Sheath**

मनोमयः कः?

मनश्च ज्ञानेन्द्रियपञ्चकं मिलित्वा यो भवति सः मनोमयः कोशः।।

*manomayaḥ kaḥ? manaśca jñānendriya-pañcakaṁ*
*militvā yo bhavati saḥ manomayaḥ kośaḥ.*

मनोमय: – mental (sheath); क: – what; मन: – mind; च – and; ज्ञानेन्द्रियपञ्चकं – the five organs of perception; मिलित्वा – together; य: – which; भवति – becomes; स: – it; मनोमय: कोश: – the mental sheath

What is mental sheath? The mind and the five organs of perception together form the mental sheath.

The mind is the seat of emotions like anger, jealousy, love, compassion and so on. It is constituted of thoughts in a state of volition. "Shall I read or not?" "Is it fun or not?" and so on. It is the mind that perceives the objects of the world through the senses. If the mind does not back the sense organs, they cannot receive any stimuli. My eyes may be open, but I miss what lies in front of me if my mind is elsewhere. The mind directs the organs of action to respond to the world.

Identified with the mental sheath, I say, "I am happy" or "I am unhappy". The Self is neither happy nor unhappy. It is of the nature of pure Bliss.

***

**The Intellectual Sheath:**

विज्ञानमय: क:?
बुद्धिर्ज्ञानेन्द्रियपञ्चकं मिलित्वा यो भवति स: विज्ञानमय: कोश:।।

*vijñānamayaḥ kaḥ? buddhir-jñānendriyapañcakaṁ militvā yo bhavati saḥ vijñānamayaḥ kośaḥ.*

विज्ञानमय: – intellectual (sheath); क: – what; बुद्धिज्ञनिन्द्रिय-पञ्चकं – the intellect and the five sense organs of perception; मिलित्वा – together; य: – which; भवति – is; स: – it; विज्ञानमय: कोश: – the intellectual sheath

What is intellectual sheath? The intellect and the five organs of perception together, is the intellectual sheath.

It is subtler than and pervades the former three sheaths. It controls the other three. It constitutes the intellect and the five organs of perception. The five senses are common to both the mental and intellectual sheaths, as perception involves both the mind and the intellect.

Thoughts in a framework of decision making is the intellect. Ignorance of the Self manifests first as the notion in the intellect as "I am a doer", "I am finite" and so on. This then gives rise to the notions, "I am tall", "I am hungry", "I am happy" and so on. Knowledge of the Self also takes place in the intellect as "I am infinite" or "I am pure happiness". The intellect is the seat of the values of life, based on which we live in the world. What we value we try to emulate, run after or cherish. If I decide that money is everything and I must have it, I act accordingly. The intellect discriminates between right and wrong, real and unreal and so on. To innovate, create, discover, visualise or imagine are intellectual abilities. The mind carries the sense perceptions to the intellect. Based on previous experience it recognises, understands and decides on the course of action. It conveys the same through the mind to the organs of action and the body prompting them into action. Hence the intellect is called the driver of the vehicle of the body.[1]

The vital air, mental and intellectual sheaths together form the subtle body.

It is good to note that during such analysis as above, the mind and intellect are categorised as two different entities. But they are two names given to thought modifications according to their functions – mind when it feels and intellect when it thinks. In common parlance they are also called the heart and the head respectively.

***

**The Bliss Sheath:**

आनन्दमयः कः?
एवमेव कारणशरीरभूताविद्यास्थमलिनसत्त्वं
प्रियादिवृत्तिसहितं सत् आनन्दमयः कोशः।
एतत् कोशपञ्चकम्।।

*ānandamayaḥ kaḥ?*
*evameva kāraṇaśarīrabhūtāvidyāstha-*
*malinasattvaṁ priyādi-vṛttisahitaṁ sat ānandamayaḥ*
*kośaḥ, etat-kośapañcakam.*

[1] *buddhiṁ tu sārathiṁ viddhi* – Kaṭhopaniṣad-1.3.3

आनन्दमय: – bliss (sheath); क: – what; एवम् – in this way; एव: – alone; कारणशरीरभूत-अविद्यास्थ-मलिनसत्त्वं – established in ignorance, which is of the form of the causal body of impure nature; प्रियादि-वृत्तिसहितं सत् – united with thoughts like priya etc.; आनन्दमय: कोश: – bliss sheath; एतत् – this; कोशपञ्चकम् – five sheaths

What is bliss sheath? Established in ignorance, which is of the form of the causal body, of impure nature, united with thoughts like priya and so on, is the bliss sheath. These are the five sheaths.

The subtlest and the most pervasive of the sheaths is the bliss sheath. It is otherwise called the causal body. It is of the nature of ignorance of the world and the Self, yet endowed with the bliss of the Self.

When night falls, the world is covered by darkness. All objects and their distinctive characterstics merge into it. The objects are not destroyed, they are just not perceived. As the day dawns, distinctions manifest. Similarly in deep sleep, when only the causal body is at play, all dualities, the ego, anxiety, agitation, the world, the subtle and gross bodies and so on, merge into total ignorance.

The cleaner and steadier the water, the sharper and brighter is the reflection of the sun. When there is total purity and stillness, the sun is reflected perfectly. Similarly, the water of the mind reflects the bliss of the Self. In the deep sleep state, as there are no thought modifications and an absence of all agitation, so the bliss of the Self manifests totally. But due to ignorance it is said to be of impure nature. Even in the waking state, the mind which is pure and calm (sāttvika) experiences greater joy than one which is agitated (rājasika) or dull (tāmasika). It should be noted that all experienced joys are reflections of the bliss of the Self alone. In the deep sleep state there are no degrees in this bliss. But in the waking and dream states, we experience various qualities and intensities of joy. There is the sāttvika joy of watching a sunrise, the rājasika joy of watching or reading a thriller and the tāmasika joy of hurting another.

The joy of thinking of a dear object or being is called priya. The intensity of joy increases when we actually gain the object or meet the person (moda). The joy is maximum when we enjoy the object or become one with it (pramoda). There is no duality of the enjoyer and the enjoyed, but only enjoyment.

The five sheaths form the covering which conceals the jewel of the Self in its folds. They are made up of or are the modifications of the five elements. They are born and so also die. They are different from 'I' the pure Self. The Self is beyond all modifications, unborn immortal and the witness of all. We are thus different from the five sheaths. This is explained in the following text:

***

## Beyond the Five Sheaths

मदीयं शरीरं मदीया: प्राणा: मदीयं मनश्च मदीया बुद्धिर्मदीयं अज्ञानमिति स्वेनैव ज्ञायते। तद्यथा मदीयत्वेन ज्ञातं कटककुण्डल–गृहादिकं स्वस्माद्भिन्नं तथा पञ्चकोशादिकं स्वस्माद्भिन्नं। मदीयत्वेन ज्ञातमात्मा न भवति।।

*madīyaṁ śarīraṁ madīyāḥ prāṇāḥ madīyaṁ manaśca madīyā buddhir-madīyaṁ ajñānamiti svenaiva jñāyate, tadyathā madīyatvena jñātaṁ kaṭaka-kuṇḍala-gṛhādikaṁ svasmād-bhinnaṁ tathā pañcakośādikaṁ svasmād-bhinnaṁ, madīyatvena jñātam-ātmā na bhavati.*

मदीयं शरीरं – my body; मदीया: प्राणा: – my prāṇas; मदीयं मन: – my mind; च – and; मदीया बुद्धि: – my intellect; मदीयं अज्ञानम् – my ignorance; इति – thus; स्वेन एव – by oneself alone; ज्ञायते – known; तद्यथा – just as; मदीयत्वेन ज्ञातं – known as mine; कटक-कुण्डल–गृहादिकं – bangles, ear-ring, house etc.; स्वस्मात् – from myself; भिन्नं – different; तथा – so also; पञ्चकोशादिक – the five sheaths etc.; स्वस्मात् – from myself; भिन्नं – different; मदीयत्वेन – as mine; ज्ञातम् – known; आत्मा – Self; न भवति – is not

Just as bangles, earrings, a house and so on, are known as 'mine' are all other than the knower, 'me'; so too, the five sheaths and so on, are known by oneself as 'my body', 'my mind', 'my intellect', and 'my ignorance' are different from me and are therefore not the Self.

An object related to 'me' is called 'my'. I am different from what I call 'my'. Also 'I' know it is 'my'. The knower is different from the known'. I say 'my wife', 'my house', 'my watch' and so on. Similarly, I say 'my body', ' my breath', 'my mind' and so on. Just as the wife and so on, are known to me , so also, the body and so on. If the wife is not me then how can the body be me?

The logic behind the fact that I am not the five sheaths is simple. But the most simple facts are the most difficult to grasp and accept. Our mind is so complicated and the habits of the past so strong that one does not see the Truth. Even if the Truth is appreciated, it is not accepted. Even if it is accepted, we do not own it. This mistake takes place, despite logic, because (a) the Self is inconceivable, therefore, we have no notion of it. It stands well-covered by the five sheaths and (b) The five sheaths are always in proximity of the Self and this makes identification with them easier.

Therefore, through continuous discrimination and firm resolve one must uncover the Self and get liberated from the shackles of the five sheaths.

# The Nature of the Self

What is the nature of the Self which is different from the three bodies, the witness of the three states and beyond the five sheaths?

आत्मा तर्हि कः? सच्चिदानन्दस्वरूपः।।

*ātmā tarhi kaḥ? saccidānandasvarūpaḥ.*

आत्मा – Self; तर्हि – then; कः – what; सत्-चित्-आनन्द-स्वरूपः – the nature of Existence-Consciousness-Bliss

Then what is the Self? It is of the nature of Existence-Consciousness-Bliss.

The not-Self (anātmā) was described in its entirety and it was explained how it is not the Self (Ātmā). The three bodies, five sheaths and the three states constitute the not-Self. Then what is the Self?

The nature of the Self can be indicated in two ways –

1. Taṭastha lakṣaṇa: Indicated with respect to the world and its conditioning as the cause of the world, the witness of the thoughts and so on.
2. Svarūpa lakṣaṇa: Indicated directly as infinite, eternal and so on.

In the following text the Self is indicated by svarūpa lakṣaṇa as Existence-Consciousness-Bliss. Each is now explained –

***

**Existence:**

सत् किम्? कालत्रयेऽपि तिष्ठतीति सत्।।

*sat kim? kālatraye'pi tiṣṭhatīti sat.*

सत् – Existence; किम् – what; कालत्रये – three periods of time; अपि – also; तिष्ठति – remains; इति – thus; सत् – is Existence

What is Existence? That which remains unchanged in the three periods of time (past, present and future) is Existence.

The past and the future are called so only with respect to the present. The Self is 'present' in all the three periods of time. It means, it was always there and will ever be. There was never a time when 'I' was not and there will never be a time when 'I' will not be there. Birth is the coming into existence of a particular name and form and death is their destruction. Since I ever exist, I am birthless (ajanmā), deathless (amara), beginningless (anādi) and endless (ananta).

Anything with a name, form and quality undergoes birth, death and change. Being birthless, I am timeless (nitya), changeless (avikāri), nameless (anāmi), formless (nirākāra) and attributeless (nirguṇa). This objectless existence is of the nature of pure Being. In it there is no becoming, as it is changeless (nirvikāra).

Everything exists because of this Existence Principle which is the very substratum of the entire universe. It is experienced in the world as the 'isness' of an object such as the book 'is', the table 'is' and so on. It is experienced within as 'I am'.

***

**Consciousness:**

चित् किम्? ज्ञानस्वरूपः।।

*cit kim? jñānasvarūpaḥ.*

चित् – Consciousness; किम् – what; ज्ञान-स्वरूपः – nature of Knowledge

What is Consciousness? It is of the nature of absolute Knowledge.

Knowledge of the world is gained as thoughts of the mind. Without thoughts, no knowledge of any object is possible. 'This is a book', 'I am hungry', 'I do not understand' and so on are thoughts of the mind. Without me the thoughts cannot be known. I illumine all my thoughts while remaining different from them. I not only illumine the presence of my thoughts, but also their absence. Thoughts come and go, but I remain unchanging and ever shining. Then who illumines the Self? None can illumine the Self. It being the subject, the Self can never be known as an object of knowledge. Also there is no need to illumine It, as it is self-shining. (The sun does not need a torchlight to illumine it.) I always know that 'I am'. I do not need anyone else to tell me so. Even in the deep sleep state when the mind is not functioning, 'I am' and I know that 'I am', as I get up saying, 'I slept well'.

This self-shining, ever shining Knowledge Principle is called Cit or Consciousness which is my true nature.

***

**Bliss:**

आनन्दः कः? सुखस्वरूपः।।

*ānandaḥ kaḥ? sukhasvarūpaḥ.*

आनन्दः – Bliss; कः – what; सुखस्वरूपः – of the nature of happiness

What is Bliss? It is of the nature of absolute happiness.

A thing is dear to me only when it gives me joy. I love my house as it is a place that gives me comfort and joy. I love myself the most. I love others for my sake, but I love myself unconditionally, totally, eternally. 'All are loved for one's sake'[1]. Therefore, I must be the source of absolute happiness.

There is sorrow in finitude. The Self is beyond time, space and objects. It is infinite and hence of the nature of absolute Bliss. Each thing tends to move towards its own nature. I always desire happiness which is my true nature.

[1] ātmanastu kāmāya sarvaṁ priyaṁ bhavati.

– *Bṛhadāraṇyaka Upaniṣad*-2.4.5

My nature is never a burden to me. Happiness is never a burden to me, whilst sorrow is.

Then why don't I experience this happiness? Why am I miserable or dissatisfied most of the time? The desires in my mind for objects veil this happiness. In moments when I am peaceful, I do experience joy within myself.

***

**In conclusion –**

एवं सच्चिदानन्दस्वरूपं स्वात्मानं विजानीयात् ।।

*evaṁ saccidānanda-svarūpaṁ svātmānaṁ vijānīyāt.*

एवम् – thus; सत्-चित्-आनन्द-स्वरूपं – the nature of Existence-Consciousness-Bliss; स्वात्मानं – of oneself; विजानीयात् – should be known

Thus one should know oneself to be of the nature of Existence-Consciousness-Bliss.

The Self is of the nature of Existence-Consciousness-Bliss. A rose is fragrant to smell, red in colour and soft to feel. The smell, colour and touch are three qualities of the same rose. However, Existence-Consciousness-Bliss are not attributes but aspects of the one Self. A quality always belongs to a substance and a substance always has a name and form. The Self is beyond all names, forms and qualities. Then are Existence, Consciousness and Bliss different from one another? The Self is partless, therefore Existence is

Consciousness and Existence-Consciousness is Bliss. The Self is infinite and there cannot be two infinites. Therefore also Existence, Consciousness and Bliss are really one. Then why are there three names? The three names indicate the nature of the Self from different standpoints. For example, With respect to the inert world, the Self is called Consciousness. However I know that 'I am' and 'I am always dear to myself'[1] is a single experience based on which I transact in the world.

We should know our infinite nature, as on knowing it, we get liberated from all sorrows for all times to come. How can we know it? The Self should be known by listening, reflecting and meditating on It[2]. One may have heard about It, reflected upon It and even attempted meditation, yet one may not realise the Self. The experience may still be only at an intellectual level (parokṣa jñāna). This is because the preparation of the mind is not sufficient. By karma-yoga, bhakti-yoga or other means the mind should be made pure, subtle and single pointed (sādhana catuṣṭaya sampanna). Knowledge gets firmly rooted in such a mind and the Self is directly experienced (aparokṣānubhūti).

---

1 ahamasmi, sadā bhāmi, kadācinnāhamapriyaḥ. – *Advaita Makaranda-2*

2 ātmā vā are draṣṭavyaḥ śrotavyo mantavyo nididhyāsitavyo.

– *Bṛhadāraṇyaka Upaniṣad*-2.4.5

# The Universe and Māyā

There are three aspects of life. The individual (jīva), the world (jagat) and the Creator (Īśvara) of the individual (microcosm) and the world (macrocosm). Every effect must have a cause. The individual and the world too, must have a cause. They are made up of the five elements. Who made the five elements? They could not have created one another, and therefore, they must have had a different cause. We call that cause Īśvara.

Having explained in detail who the individual is and what his true nature is, we now begin the discussion on the world and its true nature. It is to be noted that the individual is part of the world and cannot exist without the world.

अथ चतुर्विंशतितत्त्वोत्पत्तिप्रकारं वक्ष्यामः।।

*atha caturviṁśati-tattvotpatti-prakāraṁ vakṣyāmaḥ.*

अथ – now; चतुर्विंशति-तत्त्व-उत्पत्ति-प्रकारं – the evolution of the twenty-four factors; वक्ष्यामः – we shall explain

Now we shall explain the evolution of the twenty-four factors –

The sages counted twenty-four factors that constitute the world. They are the five great elements, (pañca-mahābhūta)

the five organs of perception, (pañca-jñānendriya), the five organs of action (pañca-karmendriya), the five prāṇas (pañca-prāṇa), and the four thought modifications (mana, buddhi, citta, ahaṅkāra). Sometimes instead of five prāṇas the five sense objects are mentioned. None of these factors – on their own or together – can be the cause of the others. Then how did the twenty-four emerge and in what order? This is explained in the following text –

***

**Māyā:**

ब्रह्माश्रया सत्त्वरजस्तमोगुणात्मिका माया अस्ति।।

*brahmāśrayā sattvarajastamo-guṇātmikā māyā asti.*

ब्रह्माश्रया – depending on Brahman; सत्त्वरजस्तमोगुणात्मिका – which is of the nature of the qualities of sattva, rajas and tamas; माया – māyā; अस्ति – is

Māyā is of the nature of the three qualities of sattva, rajas and tamas and exists depending upon Brahman.

The Truth is called Brahman (bṛhattamatvāt brahma). That which is the 'big' is Brahman. 'Big' is an adjective that generally qualifies a noun. The adjective is limited by the noun it qualifies. For example, bigness is limited to the bigness of the elephant when we say, 'This is a big elephant'. But when the adjective is used without a noun, there is no such restriction. Brahman is said to be 'the big'. Its bigness has no limits. It is infinite. We have already seen that the pure Self is infinite. Therefore, Brahman is the pure Self.

Every effect must have a cause. The world too must have a cause. The cause must exist before the effect. The Truth alone existed before the names, forms and qualities of the world came into existence. Therefore, the Truth must be the cause of the world. But the Truth is changeless. It cannot become anything other than Itself. It is of the nature of Existence-Consciousness-Bliss. But we see that the world exists, yet, it is ever-changing, inert and sorrow-ridden. Then from such a changeless cause, how can this changing world emerge?

To explain this, Vedānta postulates the concept of māyā – that which is not, yet appears to be (yā mā sā māyā). From the standpoint of the Truth, there is no world, yet we experience it. This is māyā. From the standpoint of the world, the Truth alone can be its cause, but from the standpoint of the Truth it can have no 'effect'. This is due to māyā. A snake is seen on a rope. The rope cannot create the snake, yet we experience the snake. As far as the rope is concerned, there was never a snake and there can never be a snake on it.

Māyā has two powers:

a) **The veiling power (āvaraṇa śakti):** This is of the nature of ignorance and veils the Truth. By itself this power cannot create the world.

b) **The projecting power (vikṣepa śakti):** This is the creative power that projects the entire world of names and forms. It manifests inherent impressions. It cannot do so without the veiling power. As in the previously given example, the ignorance of the rope should precede the projection of the snake vision.

The Truth when endowed with māyā is called Īśvara, the Creator of the world. Māyā, the creative power of Īśvara is worshipped in the Hindu tradition as Śakti (power). The power of māyā is unfathomable. It can make the impossible seem real. It has created this boundaryless cosmos from beginningless time and shall continue to do so endlessly. Māyā however, has no separate existence apart from the Truth. Without Existence, nothing can exist. Brahman alone has intrinsic existence. Therefore, māyā depends on the Truth for its very existence. Also in the Truth, there is no trace of māyā; therefore, māyā is destroyed upon knowing the Truth.

Māyā has three qualities. They are – sattvaguṇa characterised by knowledge, rajoguṇa which is of the nature of activity and tamoguṇa which implies inertia. These three qualities pervade the entire creation. By their permutation and combination, an infinite variety of names, forms and properties are created.

For any created object, there are two causes – the material cause (upādāna kāraṇa) and the efficient cause (nimitta kāraṇa). To make a pot there must be mud (the material cause) and the potter (the efficient cause or sentient). Usually these two causes are different from each other. The material cause remains with the object, while the efficient cause is different from the object. The mud always remains in the mud pot, but the potter makes and sells the pot. What are the material and efficient causes of the world? Are they different or the same?

The five great elements (pañcamahābhūta) are the material cause of the world. But who made them? That which made them must exist before their creation. We have already seen that the Truth alone existed before creation. Therefore, the five elements must have emerged from the Truth alone. By the same logic, the efficient cause of the world too, must be the Truth alone. We see that whenever, the material and efficient causes are the same, the created object is an illusion. For example, in the dream, the waking mind alone is the dreamworld and its creator, sustainer and destroyer. Thus, a dream is an illusion. This being so, there can be no logical sequence to creation.

However for us, the waking world is real. It does seem to be governed by natural laws and there also seems to be a cause-effect relationship between various happenings. Keeping our experience in mind, the author next explains the sequence of creation.

# The Evolution of the Five Elements

तत आकाशः संभूतः । आकाशाद् वायुः ।
वायोस्तेजः । तेजसः आपः । अद्भ्यः पृथिवी ।।

*tata ākāśaḥ sambhūtaḥ, ākāśād vāyuḥ,*
*vayostejaḥ, tejasaḥ āpaḥ, adbhyaḥ pṛthivī.*

तत – from that; आकाशः – space; संभूतः – was born; आकाशात् – from space; वायुः – air; वायोः – from air; तेजः – fire; तेजसः – from fire; आपः – water; अद्भ्यः – from water; पृथिवी – earth

From that (māyā), space was born. From space, air. From air, fire. From fire, water. From water, earth.

Māyā first created the five subtle elements, in sequence. The process of creation is from the subtle to the gross. Subtlety is measured by an object's pervasiveness and the number of perceivable qualities it has. The more pervasive the object, the more subtle it is. The lesser the number of qualities, the subtler it is. Truth is the subtlest. It is all-pervasive and beyond the cognition of any of the instruments of knowledge, as it is attributeless.

Space is the first element created by māyā. It is the subtlest of the elements. It has the quality of sound. Sound travels in the medium of space and space has an inherent sound.

From space came air, which is less pervasive. It has the qualities of sound and touch, therefore, it can be heard and felt.

Fire emerged from air. It is less pervasive than air and has the qualities of sound, touch, colour and form and it therefore, can be heard, felt and seen.

Water came next in sequence and is even less pervasive than the three mentioned above. It has the qualities of sound, touch, (colour and) form and taste and can be heard, felt, seen and tasted. Even though water is tasteless, all tastes are possible due to it.

The last emerged the earth which is the grossest and the least pervasive. It has the qualities of sound, touch, (colour and) form, taste and smell and can therefore, be heard, touched, seen, tasted and smelt.

These subtle elements are called tanmātrās. They cannot be perceived by our sense organs. Only when they become gross can they be perceived as the sense objects.

The material cause is never different from the created object. Māyā is the material cause of the five elements, and therefore, the three qualities of māyā pervade the five elements. As we have seen, the ultimate material cause of the world can be the Truth alone. Therefore, the Truth pervades the five elements, just as gold pervades all gold ornaments and water, all the waves.

When does māyā create the five elements? At the time of dissolution the three qualities of māyā remain in their unmanifest form and in a state of equilibrium (sāmya avasthā). When this balance is somehow disturbed, the process of creation begins.

# The Evolution of the Three Qualities

From the sāttvika aspect of each of the five elements are born the five organs of perception.

एतेषां पञ्चतत्त्वानां मध्ये आकाशस्य सात्त्विकांशात्
श्रोत्रेन्द्रियं संभूतम् ।
वायोः सात्त्विकांशात् त्वगिन्द्रियं संभूतम् ।
अग्नेः सात्त्विकांशात् चक्षुरिन्द्रियं संभूतम् ।
जलस्य सात्त्विकांशात् रसनेन्द्रियं संभूतम् ।
पृथिव्याः सात्त्विकांशात् घ्राणेन्द्रियं संभूतम् ।।

*eteṣāṁ pañca-tattvānāṁ madhye ākāśasya sāttvikāṁśāt*
*śrotrendriyaṁ saṁbhūtam,*
*vāyoḥ sāttvikāṁśāt tvagindriyaṁ saṁbhūtam,*
*agneḥ sāttvikāṁśāt caksurindriyaṁ saṁbhūtam,*
*jalasya sāttvikāṁśāt rasanendriyaṁ saṁbhūtam,*
*pṛthivyāḥ sāttvikāṁśat ghrāṇendriyaṁ saṁbhūtam.*

एतेषां – of these; पञ्चतत्त्वानां मध्ये – of the five elements; आकाशस्य – of space; सात्त्विकांशात् – from the sattva aspect; श्रोत्रेन्द्रियं – organ of hearing; संभूतम् – was evolved; वायोः – of air; सात्त्विकांशात् – from the sattva aspect; त्वगिन्द्रियं – organ of touch; अग्नेः – of fire; सात्त्विकांशात् – from the sattva aspect; चक्षुरिन्द्रियं – organ of sight; जलस्य – of water; सात्त्विकांशात् – from the sattva aspect;

रसनेन्द्रियं – organ of taste; पृथिव्याः – of earth; सात्त्विकांशात् – from the sattva aspect; घ्राणेन्द्रियम् – organ of smell; संभूतं – is born

From these five great elements, out of the sāttvika aspect of space, the organ of hearing, the ear, evolved. From the sāttvika aspect of air, the organ of touch, the skin, evolved. From the sāttvika aspect of fire, the organ of sight, the eye evolved. From the sāttvika aspect of water, the organ of taste, the tongue, evolved. From the sāttvika aspect of earth, the organ of smell, the nose evolved.

The subtle elements (tanmātrās) create the sense organs which also enjoy the same degree of subtlety. The main characteristic of sattvaguṇa is knowledge. Naturally, the organs of perception are born from the sāttvika aspects of the five elements. Each element has its own special quality. The corresponding sense organ is evolved to perceive its special quality. For example, from the sāttvika aspect of space, the organ of hearing is created so that it can perceive sound.

The evolution of the organs of action and perception are summarised in the following chart –

**The Organs of Action and Perception**

| Element | Sence object | Organ of perception | Deity | Function | Organ of Action | Deity | Function |
|---|---|---|---|---|---|---|---|
| Space | sound | ears | Space (Dig) | hearing | tongue | Fire (Agni) | speech |

| Element | Sence object | Organ of perception | Deity | Function | Organ of Action | Deity | Function |
|---|---|---|---|---|---|---|---|
| Air | touch | skin | Air (Vayu) | feeling | hands | Indra | grasp-ing objects |
| Fire | form | eye | Sun (Śūrya) | seeing | legs | Viṣṇu | locom-otion |
| Water | taste | tongue | Water (Varuṇa) | tasting | genitals | Prajā-pati | procr-eation |
| Earth | smell | nose | Aśvini Kumāras | smelling | anus | Death (Yama) | Elimin-ating waste |

***

The evolution of the inner equipment:

एतेषां पञ्चतत्त्वानां समष्टिसात्त्विकांशात् मनोबुद्ध्यहंकार–
चित्तान्तःकरणानि संभूतानि ।
संकल्पविकल्पात्मकं मनः । निश्चयात्मिका बुद्धिः ।
अहंकर्ता अहंकारः । चिन्तनकर्तृ चित्तम् ।
मनसो देवता चन्द्रमाः । बुद्धेः ब्रह्मा । अहंकारस्य रुद्रः ।
चित्तस्य वासुदेवः ।।

*eteṣāṁ pañcatattvānāṁ samaṣṭi-sāttvikāṁśāt*
*manobudhyahaṅkāra–cittāntaḥkaraṇāni saṁbhūtāni,*
*saṅkalpa–vikalpātmakaṁ manaḥ,*
*niścayātmikā buddhiḥ, ahaṅkartā ahaṅkāraḥ,*
*cintanakartṛ cittam, manaso devatā candramāḥ,*
*buddheḥ brahmā, ahaṅkārasya rudraḥ, cittasya vāsudevaḥ.*

एतेषां – of these; पञ्चतत्त्वानां – of the five elements; समष्टि-सात्त्विक-अंशात् - the total sāttvika aspect; मनोबुद्ध्यहंकारचित्तान्त:करणानि – the inner instruments of the mind, intellect, ego and memory; संभूतानि – are formed; संकल्प-विकल्पात्मकं – of the nature of indecision; मन: – mind; निश्चयात्मिका – the nature of decision; बुद्धि: – the intellect; अहंकर्ता – the notion of doership; अहंकार: – ego; चिन्तनकर्तृ – thinking faculty; चित्तम् – memory; मनस: – of the mind; देवता – presiding deity; चन्द्रमा: – moon; बुद्धे: – of the intellect; ब्रह्मा - Brahmā; अहंकारस्य – of the ego; रुद्र: – Rudra; चित्तस्य – of memory; वासुदेव: – Vāsudeva

From the total sāttvika aspect of these five elements the inner instruments of the mind, intellect, ego and memory are formed. The mind is of the nature of indecision. The intellect is of the nature of decision. The ego has the notion of doership. Memory is of the nature of thinking or recollection. The presiding deity of the mind is the Moon; of the intellect, Brahmā; of the ego, Rudra and of memory, Vāsudeva.

The ten organs are called the outer equipment (bahir-karaṇa) as they receive knowledge about outside objects and respond to the world. The mind receives sense perceptions, cognises them based on previous experiences and commands the senses to respond. It is called the inner equipment (antaḥkaraṇa). The mind cannot contact the world directly. It has to go through the senses. The senses also cannot function without the prompting of the mind. Hence, there is a close relationship between them. They function in coordination. Each sense organ perceives only its particular sense object. The mind receives information from all of them. It understands sound, touch, form, taste and smell. It also feels emotions and thinks thoughts. It is the seat of all knowledge, and therefore, made from the sāttvika aspect of all the five elements.

The inner equipment (antaḥkaraṇa), generally called the mind, is a continuous flow of thought modifications (vṛtti). It is classified into four according to the different functions it performs. For example, the same person is called a singer when he sings and a dancer when he dances. The four categories are:

1. **Mind (manaḥ):** Thoughts in a state of volition constitute the mind. For example, 'Should I see the movie or not? May be, I should do so tomorrow. Will I get a ticket?' Such a state of vacillation continues till a decision is made. Emotions also constitute the mind. A person dominated by his mind cannot make quick decisions and is often swayed by his emotions and moods, likes and dislikes. The moon is the presiding deity of the mind. The phases of the moon keep changing like the mind. How the moon affects the mind can be seen in a lunatic (lunar – caused by the moon) asylum. Mental disturbance in patients is seen to increase on new moon and full moon days. Most psychosomatic diseases also worsen during that time.

2. **Intellect (buddhi):** Thoughts in a state of decision constitute the intellect. Reasoning, observation, conclusion and so on, are functions of the intellect. An intellect dominated person is called a rationalist.

He or she can think logically and decisively. But one must be careful not to become a dry intellectual, bereft of tenderness. The presiding deity of the intellect is the omniscient Creator, Brahmā. All knowledge and creative ideas arise in the intellect.

3. **Ego (ahaṅkāra):** The thought, 'I am the doer', is the ego. The ego does not mean pride. It is the sense of individuality or the notion of doership. Some are proud whilst others are not, but all have the notion of doership (except a Realised person and the Lord). The mind, intellect and memory (remembered thoughts) keep changing, but the ego is there with every thought. It owns them, as 'I doubt', 'I decide', 'I remember', 'my anger', 'my idea' and so on. It comes into being with each thought. The mind, intellect and memories of each one differs, but the ego is the same. It connects the pure Self to the three bodies, five sheaths and the three states with thoughts like 'I am fat', 'I ate', and 'I slept well'. Rudra (the one who makes all cry) is the deity of the ego. Do we not suffer because of the ego? Rudra (Śiva) is the Lord of destruction. With the death of the ego, all sufferings end.

4. **Memory (cittam):** The function of cittam is the reflection and recollection. All experiences are stored as impressions and can be recollected like the data bank of a computer. We think based on this information alone. Vāsudeva (Viṣṇu) is the deity of the citta. Viṣṇu is said to wield the noble quality – sattvaguṇa. Only when we are calm and sāttvika can we clearly reflect and easily remember facts and events.

***

The Evolution of the Rajas Aspect:

एतेषां पञ्चतत्त्वानां मध्ये आकाशस्य राजसांशात् वागिन्द्रियं संभूतम् । वायोः राजसांशात् पाणीन्द्रियं संभूतम् । वह्नेः राजसांशात् पादेन्द्रियं संभूतम् । जलस्य राजसांशात् उपस्थेन्द्रियं संभूतम् । पृथिव्या राजसांशात् गुदेन्द्रियं संभूतम् । एतेषां समष्टिराजसांशात् पञ्चप्राणाः संभूताः ।।

*eteṣāṁ pañcatattvānāṁ madhye ākāśasya rājasāṁśāt vāgindriyaṁ saṁbhūtam, vāyoḥ rājasāṁśāt paṇīndriyaṁ saṁbhūtam, vahneḥ rājasāṁśāt padendriyaṁ saṁbhūtam, jalasya rājasāṁśāt upasthendriyaṁ saṁbhūtam, pṛthivyā rājasāṁśāt gudendriyaṁ saṁbhūtam, eteṣāṁ samaṣṭi-rājasāṁśāt pañcaprāṇāḥ saṁbhūtāḥ.*

एतेषां – of these; पञ्चतत्त्वानां मध्ये – of the five elements; आकाशस्य – of space; राजसांशात् – from the rājasika aspect; वागिन्द्रियं – organ of speech; संभूतम् – was formed; वायोः – of air; राजसांशात् – from the rājasika aspect; पाणीन्द्रियं – organ of grasping; संभूतम् – was formed; वह्नेः – of fire; राजसांशात् – from the rājasika aspect; पादेन्द्रियं – organ of locomotion; संभूतम् – was formed; जलस्य – of water; राजसांशात् – from the rājasika aspect; उपस्थेन्द्रियं – genital organs; संभूतं – was formed; पृथिव्याः – of earth; राजसांशात् – from the rājasika aspect; गुदेन्द्रियं – anus; संभूतम् – was formed; एतेषां – of these; समष्टि-राजसांशात् – total rājasika aspect; पञ्चप्राणाः – the five prāṇās; संभूताः – were formed

Among these five elements, from the rajas aspect of space, the organ of speech is formed. From the rajas aspect of air, the organ of grasping, the hands are formed. From the rajas aspect of fire, the organ of locomotion, the legs are formed. From the rajas aspect of water, the organ of procreation, the genitals are formed. From the rajas aspect of earth, the organ of excretion, the anus is formed. From the total rajas aspect of these five elements, the five vital airs, prāṇas are formed.

Rajoguṇa is characterised by activity. So, wherever there is activity, it is the manifestation of the rājasika aspect of māyā. The five organs of action respond to the world by activating the body and the five prāṇas supply power to all the functions of the body and keep it alive through the physiological functions. Hence, both are the manifestations of the rājasika aspect of the five elements.

The unmanifest condition of the five elements and the three qualities is the causal body. The manifestation of the sāttvika and rājasika aspect of the five elements constitutes the total subtle body or the subtle world.

***

The Evolution of the Tamas Aspect:

एतेषां पञ्चतत्त्वानां मध्ये तामसांशात् पञ्चीकृतपञ्चतत्त्वानि भवन्ति।
पञ्चीकरणं कथम् इति चेत् । एतेषां पञ्चमहाभूतानां
तामसांशस्वरूपम् एकमेकं भूतं द्विधा विभज्य एकमेकमर्धं पृथक्
तूष्णीं व्यवस्थाप्य अपरमपरमर्धं चतुर्धा विभज्य स्वार्धमन्येषु अर्धेषु
स्वभागचतुष्टयसंयोजनम् कार्यम्। तदा पञ्चीकरणं भवति।।
एतेभ्य: पञ्चीकृतपञ्चमहाभूतेभ्य: स्थूलशरीरं भवति।।

*eteṣāṁ pañcatattvānāṁ tāmasāṁśāt pañcīkṛta-pañcatattvāni bhavanti,*
*pañcīkaraṇaṁ katham iti cet, eteṣāṁ pañcamahābhūtānāṁ tāmasāṁśa-svarūpam ekam-ekaṁ bhūtaṁ dvidhā vibhajya ekam-ekam-ardhaṁ pṛthak tūṣṇīṁ vyavasthāpya aparam-aparam-ardhaṁ caturdhā vibhajya svārdham-anyeṣu ardheṣu svabhāga-catuṣṭaya-saṁyojanam kāryam, tadā pañcīkaraṇaṁ bhavati.*
*etebhyaḥ pañcīkṛta-pañcamahābhūtebhyaḥ sthūla-śarīraṁ bhavati.*

एतेषां – of these; पञ्चतत्त्वानां मध्ये - of the five elements; तामसांशात् – from the tamas aspect; पञ्चीकृतपञ्चतत्त्वानि – grossified five elements; भवन्ति – are formed; पञ्चीकरणं – pañcīkaraṇa; कथम् – how; इति चेत् – if asked; एतेषां – of these; पञ्चमहाभूतानां – of the five elements; तामसांशस्वरूपम् – from the tamas aspect; एकमेकंभूतं – each element; द्विधा विभज्य – divides into two equal parts; एकमेकंअर्धं – half of each; पृथक्– separate; तूष्णीं व्यवस्थाप्य – remaining intact; अपरम् अपरम् अर्धं – other half of each; चतुर्धा विभज्य – dividing into four equal parts; स्वार्धम् – to the intact half of its own; अन्येषु अर्धेषु स्वभागचतुष्टय – one-fourth portion of (divided) half of others (for instance, individual one-eighth portion); संयोजनम् कार्यम् – gets joined; तदा – then; पञ्चीकरणं – pañcīkaraṇam; भवति – happens; एतेभ्य: – from these; पञ्चीकृत-पञ्चमहाभूतेभ्य: – the grossified five elements; स्थूल-शरीरं – the gross body; भवति – is formed

From the tamasa aspect of these five elements, the grossified five elements are born, If it is asked how pañcīkaraṇa takes place, it is as follows: The tamasa aspect of each of the five elements divides into two equal parts. One half of each remains intact. The other half of each gets divided into four equal parts. To the intact half of one element, one-eighth portion from each of the other elements gets joined. Pañcīkaraṇa is complete. From these five grossified elements, the gross body is formed.

The chart below shows the contents of the grossified element:

| Gross | The Tamas Aspect of Subtle Elements | | | | |
|---|---|---|---|---|---|
| 1) Space (S) | 1/2 S | 1/8 A | 1/8 F | 1/8 W | 1/8 E |
| 2) Air (A) | 1/2 A | 1/8 S | 1/8 F | 1/8 W | 1/8 E |
| 3) Fire (F) | 1/2 F | 1/8 S | 1/8 A | 1/8 W | 1/8 E |
| 4) Water (W) | 1/2 W | 1/8 S | 1/8 A | 1/8 F | 1/8 E |
| 5) Earth (E) | 1/2 E | 1/8 S | 1/8 A | 1/8 F | 1/8 W |

The chart below shows the process of grossification:

| Stages | Space | Air | Fire | Water | Earth | Description |
|---|---|---|---|---|---|---|
| | 1 | 2 | 3 | 4 | 5 | |
| (i) | ◯ | ◯ | ◯ | ◯ | ◯ | Subtle elements (tanmātrās) each in itself |
| (ii) | ⊖ | ⊖ | ⊖ | ⊖ | ⊖ | Tendency to divide into two equal parts |

| Stages | Space | Air | Fire | Water | Earth | Description |
|---|---|---|---|---|---|---|
| (iii) |  |  |  |  |  | The split is complete. |
| (iv) |  |  |  |  |  | One half remaining intact the other splits into 4 |
| (v) |  |  |  |  |  | Each half combines with one bit of other four elements |

Tamoguṇa is characterised by inertia. Inert means that which cannot know itself or illumine another. That which cannot activate itself is inert. The tāmasika aspect of the five elements together undergo the process of grossification as explained in the charts. By their intermingling, each element thereafter, has 50% of its own element and 12.5% of each of the other four. Therefore each of the gross elements has the qualities of all the other elements. These elements thereafter are perceived by the senses. The permutation and combination of these elements form the entire gross world including the gross body.

The vegetables we eat have starch, proteins and vitamins (earth), water content, its own heat, air and occupies space. Even though water in its purest form is supposed to be tasteless, colourless and odourless, we know that sea water tastes salty, appears blue and has a distinct smell. Our own body occupies space. We have plenty of air within us. The body has heat and around 70% of it is made up of water. There is the earth (food) element, which makes up most of its weight.

The gross body cannot function without the subtle body. When the subtle body leaves the gross body, the gross body disintegrates and merges into the five gross elements. As all the gross bodies have the same gross elements and no gross body can claim to be superior to another from the standpoint of the contents of the body. The proverbial blue blood is also red. Differences at the gross level are superficial. If this is understood, then conflicts due to caste, creed, colour or gender would end.

# The Relationship of the Individual and the Lord

The whole universe has emerged from Māyā which is inherent in the Truth. Then how are the individuals related to the Truth?

एवं पिण्डब्रह्माण्डयोरैक्यं संभूतम्।।

*evaṁ piṇḍabrahmāṇḍayor-aikyaṁ saṁbhūtaṁ.*

एवं – in this way; पिण्ड-ब्रह्माण्डयोः – of the microcosm and macrocosm; ऐक्यं – identity; संभूतम् – is established

Thus, there is identity (oneness) between the microcosm and the macrocosm.

The part is never separate from the whole. It is always inherent in the whole. Minus a single part, the whole is not complete, therefore not whole.

The individual subtle body is made from the total subtle elements. For instance, the individual mind is part of the total mind. Similarly, the individual gross body is made from the total gross elements. Therefore, the individual gross body (piṇḍa) is part of the total gross body (brahmāṇḍa). So the individual and the Total enjoy a part-whole relationship. However, the original cause of the total gross and subtle elements is the Truth, the pure Self. The cause pervades the effects. Therefore, in essence, there is identity between the individual and the Total. The waves are only part of the ocean in terms of name and form. But with respect to their essence, the water, they are one.

***

This essential oneness is explained further thus:

स्थूलशरीराभिमानि जीवनामकं ब्रह्मप्रतिबिम्बं भवति।
स एव जीवः प्रकृत्या स्वस्मात् ईश्वरं भिन्नत्वेन जानाति।
अविद्योपाधिः सन् आत्मा जीव इत्युच्यते।
मायोपाधिः सन् ईश्वर इत्युच्यते।
एवम् उपाधिभेदात् जीवेश्वरभेददृष्टिः यावत् पर्यन्तं तिष्ठति
तावत् पर्यन्तं जन्ममरणादिरूपसंसारो न निवर्तते।
तस्मात्कारणात् न जीवेश्वरयोर्भेदबुद्धिः स्वीकार्या।।

*sthūlaśarīrābhimāni jīvanāmakaṁ brahma-pratibimbaṁ bhavati, sa eva jīvaḥ prakṛtyā svasmāt īśvaraṁ bhinnatvena jānāti, avidyopādhiḥ san ātmā jīva ityucyate, māyopādhiḥ san īśvara ityucyate, evam upādhi-bhedāt jīveśvara-bheda-dṛṣṭiḥ yāvat paryantaṁ tiṣṭhati tāvat paryantaṁ janma-maraṇādirūpa-saṁsāro na nivartate, tasmāt-kāraṇāt na jīveśvarayor-bheda-buddhiḥ svīkāryā.*

स्थूलशरीर–अभिमानि – one who identifies with the gross body; जीवनामकं – called the jīva; ब्रह्मप्रतिबिम्बं – reflection of Brahman (Truth); भवति – is; सः – that; एव – alone; जीवः – individual;

प्रकृत्या – by nature; स्वस्मात् – from himself; ईश्वरं – the Lord; भिन्नत्वेन – as different; जानाति – considers; अविद्योपाधि: सन् – conditioned by ignorance; आत्मा – the Self; जीव: – individual; इति – thus; उच्यते – is called; मायोपाधि: सन् – conditioned by māyā; ईश्वर – Lord (Īśvara); इत्युच्यते – is called; एवम् – in this way; उपाधिभेदात् – due to difference in conditionings; जीवेश्वरभेददृष्टि: – the vision of difference between individual and the Lord (jīva and Īśvara); यावत् पर्यन्तं – as long as; तिष्ठति – remains; तावत्पर्यन्तं – so long; जन्ममरणादिरूप-संसार: – saṁsāra which is of the nature of birth, death and so on; न निवर्तते – is not removed; तस्मात् कारणात् – for that reason; जीवेश्वरयो: – of the individual and the Lord (jīva and Īśvara); भेदबुद्धि: – difference; न स्वीकार्या – should not be accepted

The reflection of Truth (Brahman), which identifies with the gross body is called the individual (jīva). This individual by nature considers the Lord (Īśvara) to be essentially different from himself/herself. The Self (ātmā), conditioned by ignorance (avidyā) is called the individual and when conditioned by māyā is called the Lord. Their difference is due to the conditionings. So long as the notion that the individual and the Lord are essentially different remains, till then there is no redemption from the saṁsāra which is in the form of repeated birth, death and so on. Due to that reason, the notion that the individual is essentially different from the Lord should not be accepted.

The Truth (Brahman) is infinite. It wields its inherent creative power, the total conditioning, māyā, and appears as the world of things and beings. Truth with the conditioning of māyā is called the Lord (Īśvara). As the Creator, Sustainer and Destroyer of the world, He is all-powerful (sarvaśaktimān), all-knowing (sarvajñaḥ) and all-pervading (sarvavyāpī). He is both the material and efficient cause of the world. The Lord always knows His true nature and does not get overpowered by māyā. He remains in full control of māyā and is thus called the Lord of Māyā (Māyāpati). His māyā is predominantly sāttvika, and therefore, does not bind. So, when one takes refuge in Him, one gets liberated from māyā[1].

The same infinite Truth, when wielding the individual conditioning (avidyā) is called the individual (jīva). Avidyā being predominantly tāmasika and of the nature of ignorance, binds the individual. He identifies with the finite gross and subtle bodies and lives as a finite creature, helpless, hopeless and sorrowful forgetting his infinite nature. He is enslaved by his conditionings, and therefore, called māyādāsa.

The sun reflects in a bucket of water and assumes a small identity as a reflection in the water. The reflection is conditioned by the bucket and the state of the water. If the reflection forgets its true nature of infinite light, it feels bound by the bucket of water. If it realises that it is light alone, then it plays around in the water, unaffected. Similarly, Truth reflected in the bucket of the gross body and the waters of the subtle body is called the individual (jīva). He forgets his true nature and thinks he is the body. Thereafter, he thinks that every other object and being is

[1] māmeva ye prapadyante māyāmetāṁ taranti te. – *Gītā*-7.14

different from himself and the Lord (Īśvara) to be someone far away from him. This vision, born of ignorance, is so deeply rooted that even when told that he is not finite, he does not accept it. This false identification and notion of difference has been with him from beginningless time, birth after birth. In fact, it is the cause of the endless births that he goes through.

Man desires to be complete, be happy and exist forever. He therefore, runs after that which he thinks will make him happy. Actions give results. Those results when enjoyed or suffered, cause impressions which again give rise to desires. Thus continues the cycle of birth and death. This ends only when we realise that 'I am what I seek'. Knowing myself to be infinite Existence-Consciousness-Bliss would liberate me from the cycle of transmigration.

Therefore, we are advised not to accept this ignorance born difference between the individual and the Lord and realise their essential identity.

# Enquiry into the Statement – That Thou Art

The essential oneness of the individual and the Lord is realised through enquiry into the statement - That Thou Art.

ननु साहंकारस्य किंचिज्ज्ञस्य जीवस्य निरहंकारस्य सर्वज्ञस्य
ईश्वरस्य तत्त्वमसीति महावाक्यात् कथमभेदबुद्धिः स्यादुभयोः
विरुद्धधर्माक्रान्तत्वात्।।

*nanu sāhaṁkārasya kiñcijjñasya jīvasya nirahaṁkārasya sarvajñasya īśvarasya tat-tvam-asīti mahāvākyāt katham-abheda-buddhiḥ syād-ubhayoḥ viruddha-dharmākrāntatvāt.*

ननु – but; साहंकारस्य – of one with ego; किंचिज्ज्ञस्य – of one with limited knowledge; जीवस्य – of the individual; निरहंकारस्य – of one without ego; सर्वज्ञस्य ईश्वरस्य – of one who is the omniscient Lord; तत् – That; त्वम् – you; असि – are; इति महावाक्यात् – the great statement; कथम् – how; अभेदबुद्धिः – vision of oneness; स्यात् – is; उभयोः – of the two; विरुद्धधर्माक्रान्तत्वात् – being of opposite natures

But the individual is endowed with ego and his knowledge is limited, whereas, the Lord is without ego and is omniscient. Then how can there be identity, as stated in the great statement – 'That thou art', between these two, who are possessed of contradictory characteristics?

The very goal of human life is to realise one's own true nature and the very purpose of the Vedas is to gain the knowledge of the Self. The statements in the Vedas that indicate the unity of the individual and the infinite Truth are called Mahāvākyas – great statements. Many such statements are found in the Vedas, but four of them (one from each Veda) are very famous. One amongst them is 'tattvamasi' meaning – 'That thou art'. It is found in the Chāndogya Upaniṣad Chapter 6 of the Sāma Veda in a dialogue between Sage Uddālaka and his disciple Śvetaketu. The Guru explains that the Truth alone existed before creation. From It emerged the entire creation like gold ornaments from gold. That Truth (tat) alone are (asi) you (tvam), states sage Uddālaka.

Some people are shocked at hearing this seeming blasphemous statement that the Lord, Īśvara, and I are one. Others dismiss it as exaggeration used in praise of the individual. Some others feel that what is meant herein is that the individual is like the Lord, as he has inherited certain characteristics of Him. However what is actually meant in the Upaniṣad is that there is total identity or oneness between the two. How is that possible?

The individual as we know, is finite, with limited knowledge (alpajña), limited strength (alpa śaktimān), is like a dot in the universe (alpavyāpi), is deluded by māyā (māyādāsa), is dependent upon the world for everything, helplessly entangled in actions and full of sorrows and problems. The Lord, on the other hand, is infinite, omniscient (sarvajña), all strength (sarvaśaktimān), all-pervading (sarvavyāpi), controls māyā (māyāpati), is independent of actions and is unaffected by results of actions and is all joy.

***

How can the finite ever be one with the Infinite? How can two entities with such opposite characteristics ever be one? The question is answered thus:

इति चेन्न। स्थूलसूक्ष्मशरीराभिमानी त्वंपदवाच्यार्थः
उपाधिविनिर्मुक्तं समाधिदशा-संपन्नं शुद्धं चैतन्यं त्वंपद-लक्ष्यार्थः।
एवं सर्वज्ञत्वादि-विशिष्ट ईश्वरः तत्पद-वाच्यार्थः।
उपाधिशून्यं शुद्धचैतन्यं तत्पद-लक्ष्यार्थः।
एवं च जीवेश्वरयोः चैतन्यरूपेणाभेदे बाधकाभावः॥

*iti cenna, sthūlasūkṣma-śarīrābhimānī tvaṁ-
pada-vācyārthaḥ upādhi-vinirmuktaṁ samādhi-daśā-
saṁpannaṁ śuddhaṁ caitanyaṁ tvaṁpada-lakṣyārthaḥ,
evaṁ sarvajñatvādi-viśiṣṭa īśvaraḥ tatpada-vācyārthaḥ,
upādhiśūnyaṁ śuddha-caitanyaṁ tatpada-lakṣyārthaḥ,
evaṁ ca jīveśvarayoḥ caitanyarūpeṇābhede bādhakābhāvaḥ.*

इति चेत् – if asked thus; न – no; स्थूल-सूक्ष्म-शरीर-अभिमानी – one identified with the gross and subtle bodies; त्वंपदवाच्यार्थः – literal meaning of the word 'thou'; उपाधिविनिर्मुक्तं – free from all conditionings; समाधिदशासंपन्नं – in the state of deep meditation; शुद्धं – pure; चैतन्यं – Consciousness; त्वंपदलक्ष्यार्थः – is the implied meaning of thou; एवं – in the same way; सर्वज्ञत्वादि-विशिष्टः – one endowed with omniscience, etc.; ईश्वरः – The Lord; तत्पदवाच्यार्थः – is the literal meaning of the word

'That'; उपाधिशून्यं – free from all conditionings; शुद्धचैतन्यं – pure Consciousness; तत्पदलक्ष्यार्थ: – that is the implied meaning of the word 'That'; एवं – thus; च – and; जीवेश्वरयो: – of the individual and the Lord; चैतन्यरूपेण – from the standpoint of Awareness; अभेदे बाधक-अभाव: – there is no contradiction in their essential oneness

If there is such a doubt, no (it is not so). The literal meaning of the word 'thou' is the one identified with the gross and subtle bodies. The implied meaning of the word 'thou' is pure Consciousness which is free from all conditionings and which is appreciated in the state of deep meditation. So also the literal meaning of the word 'That' is the Lord who is endowed with omniscience, etc. The implied meaning of the word 'That' is the pure Consciousness free from all conditionings. Thus, there is no contradiction regarding the essential oneness between the individual and the Lord from the standpoint of Consciousness.

It is understandable that the student cannot accept that the individual and the Lord are one. As the vision, so the world and the Lord appear to us. (yathā dṛṣṭiḥ tathā sṛṣṭiḥ). To a villager the town is big, but to the urban dweller it is small. Similarly, when we look at Īśvara from the standpoint of our conditioning, we can see only the conditioning of the Lord and therefore, conclude that we are different from Him. Bhagavān Ramana Maharshi was asked if the Lord was with or without form and qualities. He said, 'It depends on what you think you are. If you think you are with form, He too, is with form. If you think you are formless, then He too, being formless, is one with you'.

A sentence has two meanings:

1) The literal meaning (vācyārtha): Herein each word is understood literally and put together as a sentence to give us a particular meaning. For example, 'The dog barks'.

2) The indicative meaning (lakṣyārtha): Herein the literal meaning is rejected and the implied meaning is understood. For example, 'He is a lion'. This sentence does not mean that the man is literally a lion but that he is brave like a lion. The statement 'That thou art', should not be taken literally but in its implied sense.

The literal meaning of 'thou' is the individual identified with the three bodies, the three states and the five sheaths. This gives rise to the notion, 'I am a changing, finite entity'. When the Self, free from all conditionings is experienced, I realise that, 'I am Existence-Consciousness-Bliss'. This state of realisation is called samādhi. Similarly from the standpoint of the conditioning, of the totality the Lord is the creator, sustainer and destroyer of the universe. Free of all the conditionings of māyā, He is in essence Existence-Consciousness-Bliss. Thus, in essence, the individual and the Lord are one. This is realised only when our attention shifts from the conditionings to the unconditioned Self or Truth. The enquiry may start either from the Lord as to who He is in essence or it may start with the individual with the question, 'Who am I in essence?' Either way it culminates in the realisation, 'I am the Infinite Truth – ahaṁ brahmāsmi'.

# Man of Realisation

The following text explains who is a Man of Realisation.

एवं च वेदान्तवाक्यैः सद्गुरूपदेशेन च सर्वेष्वपि भूतेषु येषां ब्रह्मबुद्धिरुत्पन्ना ते जीवन्मुक्ताः इत्यर्थः।।

*evaṁ ca vedānta-vākyaiḥ sadgurūpadeśena ca sarveṣvapi bhūteṣu yeṣāṁ brahma-buddhir-utpannā te jīvanmuktāḥ ityarthaḥ.*

एवं – thus; च – and; वेदान्तवाक्यैः – by the words of Vedānta; सद्गुरु-उपदेशेन – by the teaching of the Sadguru; च – and; सर्वेषु अपि – in all; भूतेषु – beings; येषां – whose; ब्रह्मबुद्धिः – vision of Truth; उत्पन्ना – is born; ते – they; जीवन्मुक्ताः – Liberated while living; इत्यर्थः – is meant

Thus by the words of Vedānta and the teachings of the Sadguru, those in whom the vision of the Truth is born in all beings, are Liberated while living (jīvanmuktāḥ).

The words of Vedānta reveal our true nature. Since the Self cannot be known as an object of knowledge, it has to be revealed by subtle and indicative methods. The language used in the Vedas is therefore, mystical. The teacher adopts a method best suited for the student he teaches. He understands the mind of the student and lifts him up gradually to the highest Truth. It is to be noted that the Guru can only indicate the Truth. The student has to lift his mind by himself (uddharet-ātmanātmānam). Therefore, Vedānta, as revealed by the Guru, is the means for Self-realisation. If one were to read the Vedas independently, one would get hopelessly lost and confused. One would not be able to resolve the apparent contradictions and would either conclude wrongly, or give up, thinking that it is too difficult or illogical. When the student listens, especially a qualified one (sādhana-catuṣṭaya-sampanna), to the words of the Sadguru who is well-versed in the scriptures (śrotriya) and well establised in the Truth (brahmaniṣṭha), he realises the Truth. He realises that the Self in him is the Self in all (madātmā sarvabhūtātmā), that all is Truth alone (sarvaṁ khalu idaṁ brahma); that I am the Infinite Reality (ahaṁ brahmāsmi). Such a person is called a jīvanmukta – one Liberated whilst living.

***

We are naturally interested in knowing more about such a mind-blowing state and about one who revels in that state. So the text continues with the question:

ननु जीवन्मुक्तः कः?
यथा देहोऽहं पुरुषोऽहं ब्राह्मणोऽहं शूद्रोऽहमस्मीति
दृढनिश्चयस्तथा नाहं ब्राह्मणः न शूद्रः न पुरुषः किन्तु असंगः
सच्चिदानन्दस्वरूपः प्रकाशरूपः सर्वान्तर्यामी चिदाकाश-
रूपोऽस्मीति दृढनिश्चयरूपोऽपरोक्षज्ञानवान् जीवन्मुक्तः।।

*nanu jīvanmuktaḥ kaḥ?*
*yathā deho'haṁ puruṣo'haṁ*
*brāhmaṇo'haṁ śūdro'ham-asmīti dṛḍhaniścayas-*
*tathā nāhaṁ brāhmaṇaḥ na śūdraḥ na puruṣaḥ*
*kintu asaṅgaḥ saccidānanda-svarūpaḥ prakāśarūpaḥ*
*sarvāntaryāmī cidākāśarūpo'smīti dṛḍhaniścaya-*
*rūpo'parokṣa-jñānavān jīvanmuktaḥ.*

ननु – then; जीवन्मुक्तः – one Liberated while living; कः – who; यथा – just as; देहः अहं – I am the body; पुरुषः अहं – I am a man; ब्राह्मणोऽहं – I am a Brāhmaṇa; शूद्रः अहम् अस्मि – I am a śūdra; इति – thus; दृढनिश्चयः – firm belief; तथा – in the same way; न अहं ब्राह्मणः – I am not a Brāhmaṇa; न शूद्रः – I am not a śūdra; न पुरुषः – not a man; किन्तु – but; असंगः – unattached; सच्चिदानन्द स्वरूपः – of the nature of Existence-Consciousness-Bliss; प्रकाशरूपः – effulgent; सर्वान्तर्यामी – the indweller of all; चिदाकाशरूपः अस्मि – I am the formless Awareness; इति – thus; दृढनिश्चयः – firm determination; अपरोक्षज्ञानवान् – one with immediate knowledge; जीवन्मुक्तः – one Liberated while living

Then who is the one Liberated while living? Just as we have firm belief that 'I am the body', 'I am a man', I am a Brāhmaṇa' or 'I am a śūdra', in the same way one who, by his immediate knowledge (aparokṣa jñāna) has firmly ascertained 'I am not a Brāhmaṇa', 'I am not a śūdra', 'I am not a man' but 'I am unattached and of the nature of Existence-Consciousness-Bliss, effulgent, the indweller of all and the formless Awareness', is one Liberated while living.

Presently for us, the knowledge that I am a human being, moreover, a man or woman, is natural and effortless. I get up each morning with this thought and sleep with it. It will remain with me till I die. It is not merely a thought; all actions too, are based on this notion. Further, it is not a conscious thought. I do not have to meditate or repeat 'I am a man' each morning. I do not need anyone to remind me that I am a man. I do not even have to remind myself. This knowledge is firmly rooted in me and despite being told and intellectually convinced that I am not the body, I still conduct my life with the knowledge 'I am a man'.

When the knowledge 'I am not the body', but 'I am pure, infinite Awareness' becomes firmly rooted and effortless, a person is called one Liberated while living. He need not meditate or remind himself about his true nature. This knowledge stays with him under all circumstances. Even at the time of death of the body, he knows that he is the immortal Self. He may even appear to be very ordinary, but his vision is quite the opposite of the ignorant man! The ignorant person takes himself to be the finite, transmigrating individual and the world to be real. The Liberated one knows himself to be the infinite Self and the world to be unreal.

**asaṅga:** The Self, being different from the three bodies and three states, is totally unaffected by them. So too, the liberated one is unattached to them and the world. Remaining unattached, he moves like the wind (asaktaḥ vāyuvat caret).

**Saccidānanda svarūpa:** The Self is ever existent, the witness of all and infinite. The Liberated one therefore, has no fear of death and suffers from no limitations.

**prakāśarūpa:** The Self is the Knowledge Principle that illumines all thoughts, the Life Principle that enlivens all beings.

**sarvāntaryāmī:** The Liberated one knows that the Self in me is the Self in all. He therefore loves all as his own Self. Tulasīdāsajī says, "siyarāma main sabajaga jāni, karauṁ praṇāma jori juga pāni". Knowing that the entire world is pervaded by my Lord (Siyā-Rāma), with folded hands, I prostrate to all.

**cidākāśa:** Space is all-pervading. The Self pervades even space, i.e. it is beyond space. It is the very illuminator of the concept of space.

Knowledge is of three types:

1. **pratyakṣa-jñāna** – Direct knowledge: It is that which is known directly by our sense organs. For example, I see this book.

2. **parokṣa-jñāna** – Indirect knowledge: It is that which is gained by hearing from others or reading. It is knowledge of an object faraway that is not in the reach of the senses. Direct knowledge can become indirect knowledge and vice versa. For example, I had never seen the Taj Mahal, but had heard of it; now I am seeing it. My home is now far away and I do not perceive it.

3. **aparokṣa-jñāna** – Immediate knowledge: It is that which is neither direct nor indirect, as it is not of an object which is either near or far. The knowledge of the Subject 'I' is always immediate. No means of knowledge like the senses and mind are needed to know myself. We all know 'I am', but we do not know our true nature. The Liberated one knows who he is in his true nature. His knowledge is not merely an intellectual concept, but an immediate experience 'I am infinte Self/Truth'.

***

What is the purpose of this knowledge? What do I gain from it? This is explained as follows:

ब्रह्मैवाहमस्मीत्यपरोक्षज्ञानेन निखिलकर्मबन्धविनिर्मुक्तः स्यात्।।

*brahmaivāham-asmītyaparokṣajñānena*
*nikhila-karmabandha-vinirmuktaḥ syāt.*

ब्रह्म-एव-अहम्-अस्मि-इति – I am Brahman alone; अपरोक्षज्ञानेन – by immediate knowledge; निखिलकर्मबन्धविनिर्मुक्तः स्यात् – one becomes free from bondage of all karmas

By the immediate knowledge 'I am Brahman alone', one becomes free from the bondage of all karmas (actions).

By immediate knowledge of the Self, one does not gain any special powers, unworldly experiences or worldly achievements. One need not stop performing worldly actions or do something extraordinary. Knowledge does not create anything new, it only removes the ignorance of the Self. The false notion that I am finite is removed. The ignorant man performs actions with the notion that 'I am the doer (kartā)' and therefore, he becomes the enjoyer and sufferer (bhoktā) of the results. The Realised soul knows that he is neither the doer of actions (akartā), nor the enjoyer of results (abhoktā) and is therefore free from the bondage of actions.

Also, having attained supreme Bliss, there is nothing more to be attained (prāptavya) and therefore, there remains nothing more to be done (kartavya). He may perform duties, but he does so with complete detachment. We perform actions compelled from within by a sense of incompleteness. The Liberated one performs actions out of a sense of fulfilment and with love for all. He does not seek freedom from action, as he experiences freedom even in action.

# Actions and Freedom from Bondage in Actions

There are three types of results of action. They are -

कर्माणि कतिविधानि सन्तीति चेत् आगामिसञ्चित-
प्रारब्धभेदेन त्रिविधानि सन्ति।।

*karmāṇi katividhāni santīti cet āgāmi-sañcita-*
*prārabdha-bhedena trividhāni santi.*

कर्माणि – actions; कतिविधानि – how many types; सन्ति – are; इति चेत् – if asked thus; आगामि-सञ्चित-प्रारब्धभेदेन – āgāmi, sañcita and prārabdha; त्रिविधानि – three kinds; सन्ति – are there

If it is asked, 'How many kinds of karmas are there?', (the reply is) There are three kinds of karmas, viz. āgami, sañcita and prārabdha.

Can we live without actions? Even to keep the body alive, one has to act. Man performs countless actions from birth to death. Each action produces results. The various actions are categorised into three, depending upon the result that one gets from them at different periods of time. They are āgāmi, sañcita and prārabdha. Each of them is explained as follows:

## Āgāmi Karma

**ज्ञानोत्पत्त्यनन्तरम् ज्ञानिदेहकृतं पुण्यपापरूपं कर्म यदस्ति तदागामीत्यभिधीयते।।**

*jñānotpattyanantaraṁ jñāni-dehakṛtaṁ puṇya-pāpa-rūpam karma yadasti tadāgāmītyabhidhīyate.*

ज्ञानोत्पत्त्यनन्तरम् – after the dawn of Knowledge; ज्ञानिदेहकृतं – done by the body of the Realised Soul; पुण्यपापरूपं – of the nature of merit and demerit; कर्म – actions; यद् – which; अस्ति – are; तद् – that; आगामि – āgāmi; इति – thus; अभिधीयते – known

The results of actions, good or bad performed by the body of the Realised Soul (jñāni) after the dawn of knowledge are known as āgāmi.

What you sow today, you reap tomorrow. The results of what you do today come as āgāmi karmas in the future. The results may come either in the next instant, after a few years or in a future life. The results get drawn to the performer of the action. It may appear that one acts, while the other enjoys or suffers the results but the doer alone becomes the enjoyer and sufferer of the results.

Animals too are identified with the body but perform actions without a sense of doership. They have no choice in action but act according to instincts, as programmed by nature or God. Man, having identified with the body, acts with a sense of doership and has a choice in action. He may do, may not do, or do otherwise (kartum śakyam akartum śakyam anyathā vā kartum śakyam). A wise man, not being identified with his body, has no sense of doership, yet may appear to be performing actions through his body. As far as he is concerned, he is the pure Self, free from actions.

The results of actions depend upon the intention behind the actions. Good intentions result in merit (puṇya) and bad in demerit (pāpa). Those which result in sorrow, tension, regret or guilt are pāpa karmas, whilst those that give joy, a feeling of inner fulfilment and self-congratulation are called puṇya karmas. Actions which spring from a concern and love for others and is one's own duty are meritorious actions (puṇya karmas). Those which spring from selfish motives and are prohibited are sins (pāpa karmas). Sometimes it is difficult to determine exactly what constitutes meritorious actions or sins, duties or prohibited actions. One must always be alert and perform only good actions if one wishes to live peacefully. But as far as a wise man is concerned, there are no good or bad actions for him as he has no sense of doership.

**Sañcita Karma**

सञ्चितं कर्म किम्?
अनन्तकोटिजन्मनां बीजभूतं सत् यत्कर्मजातं पूर्वार्जितं तिष्ठति
तत् सञ्चितं ज्ञेयम्।।

*sañcitaṁ karma kim? anantakoṭi-janmanāṁ*
*bīja-bhūtaṁ sat yatkarmajātaṁ pūrvārjitaṁ tiṣṭhati*
*tat sañcitaṁ jñeyam.*

सञ्चितं कर्म – sañcita karma; किम् – what; अनन्तकोटिजन्मनां – of endless births; बीजभूतं – in the seed form; सत् – being; यत् – which; कर्मजातं – results of actions; पूर्वार्जितं – gained from the past; तिष्ठति – remains; तत् – that; सञ्चितं – sañcita; ज्ञेयम् – should be known

The results of actions performed in (all) previous births which are in seed form and giving rise to endless crores of births (in future), are called sañcita (accumulated) karma.

The word 'sañcita' comes from the verbal root 'ci' which means to collect (sañcita – that which is well collected). The individual (jīva) from beginningless time has taken innumerable births in various bodies, besides the human body, in which he exhausts his stock of karmas, but does not create any new karmas. But in the human birth, he not only exhausts but also creates new karmas. These actions done in the present which get accumulated to our account and are to be enjoyed in future births, are called sañcita karmas. Each one of us already has a very good capital of karma and we are constantly adding to it. This capital is enough to give us endless births in various bodies.

If man learns the knack of performing right actions with the right attitude, he would be able to exhaust his karmas without creating new ones for future enjoyment. Even if he collects karmas, he should be careful to collect only those that would give him happiness in the future and take him to higher realms.

**Prārabdha Karma**

प्रारब्धं कर्म किमिति चेत्।
इदं शरीरमुत्पाद्य इह लोके एव सुखदुःखादिप्रदं यत्कर्म तत्प्रारब्धम्।
भोगेन नष्टं भवति। प्रारब्धकर्मणां भोगादेव क्षय इति।।

*prārabdhaṁ karma kimiti cet, idaṁ śarīram-utpādya*
*iha loke eva sukha-duḥkhādipradaṁ yatkarma*
*tatprārabdham, bhogena naṣṭaṁ bhavati,*
*prārabdha-karmaṇāṁ bhogādeva kṣaya iti.*

प्रारब्धं कर्म – prārabdha karma; किम् – what; इति चेत् – if asked thus; इदं – this; शरीरम् उत्पाद्य – body having created; इह – this; लोके – world; एव – alone; सुखदुःखादिप्रदं – gives joy, sorrow and so on; यत् – which; कर्म – actions; तत् – that; प्रारब्धम् – is prārabdha; भोगेन – by enjoying; नष्टं – destroyed; भवति – becomes; प्रारब्धकर्मणां – of prārabdha karma; भोगात् – through enjoyment; एव – alone; क्षयः – exhaustion; इति – thus

Having given birth to this body, the actions which give result in this very world in the form of happiness or misery and which can be destroyed only by enjoying (or suffering) them is called prārabdha karma.

That which has started well is called prārabdha (pra+ārabdha). From the total capital of karmas (sañcita), those actions which have fructified to give us the present birth and the experiences in this birth are prārabdha karmas. Prārabdha decides the time and place of our birth, the environment in which we live, our lifespan and so on. It is commonly called fate, destiny or luck. One should not think of prārabdha with a negative connotation as – 'God has decided my fate. Now I am helpless. I will have to go through it. There is no use in doing anything as everything is decided, we can't change anything.' In fact, by understanding that what I get now is because of what I have done in the past, I stop blaming others and take full responsibility for my life and experiences. The understanding that I deserve what I get, makes us strive to deserve better. We may have no choice in what we get, but we do have a choice in the attitude with which we receive it and in what we do with what we get. Pūjya Swami Chinmayananda said, "What I get is His gift to me, what I do with what I get is my gift to Him."

A fruit reaches its full maturity and then disintegrates. An arrow that has been shot from the bow, hits its target and exhausts its momentum. Once shot cannot be withdrawn halfway. Similarly, those actions which have started fructifying get exhausted only by giving their results. One has to go through the results of one's actions, whether one likes them or not. These results come to us as conducive or unconducive situations. A wise man too, has taken birth in his body due to his prārabdha karmas. Even after attaining Knowledge, the prārabdha of the body continues. We therefore, see that even a wise man may get cancer or a heart attack. As far as he is concerned, he remains the non-doer and non-enjoyer. But from the standpoint of the ignorant he too, is seen to undergo various conducive and unconducive situations. The bodies of the ignorant as well as that of the wise man finally get destroyed.

***

What happens to the sañcita karma of a Realised Master?

सञ्चितं कर्म ब्रह्मैवाहमिति निश्चयात्मकज्ञानेन नश्यति।।

*sañcitaṁ karma brahmaivāhamiti niścayātmaka-jñānena naśyati.*

सञ्चितं कर्म – sañcita karma; ब्रह्म एव अहम् – I am the Truth (Brahman) alone; इति – thus; निश्चयात्मक-ज्ञानेन – by the firm knowledge; नश्यति – is destroyed

Sañcita karma is destroyed by the firm knowledge, 'I am the Truth (Brahman) alone'.

A man commits many crimes and is wanted by the law for them. There are many criminal cases pending against him in the courts. But when he dies, the file is closed. The one who committed those crimes is no more available to be punished. Similarly, the finite individual who identifies with the body, owns all its actions, collects them, and later enjoys or suffers their results in the present and future births. This feeling of finitude is born from the ignorance of one's true nature. On gaining the knowledge, 'I am the infinite Consciousness', the false notion that 'I am the finite, changing, suffering entity' is destroyed. There remains no individuality that owns actions or identifies with the body to enjoy or suffer them. Therefore, the entire capital of actions becomes null and void. It cannot give results. It is compared to roasted seeds. Once roasted, they can no longer sprout.

At death the gross body of the ignorant and that of the wise disintegrates to merge with the five gross elements. The subtle body of the ignorant man propelled by the causal body or the force of previous actions, leaves the gross body to take up a new body according to the results of actions that have fructified. The subtle body of the wise man merges with its five subtle elements as there is no propelling force to give it direction or hold it together. The causal body, the cause of the gross and subtle bodies of the wise man, is destroyed by the knowledge of the Self. There is no more birth for him. For example, space appears to be conditioned by a pot. Once the pot breaks, the pot space merges with the total space. There is no actual merging. Space was always one and all-pervading, even when the pot existed.

***

What happens to the āgāmi karmas of a Realised Master?

आगामि कर्म अपि ज्ञानेन नश्यति किञ्च आगामिकर्मणां
नलिनीदलगतजलवत् ज्ञानिनां सम्बन्धो नास्ति।।

*āgāmi karma api jñānena naśyati kiñca āgāmi-karmaṇāṁ nalinīdalagata-jalavat jñānināṁ sambandho nāsti.*

आगामि कर्म – āgāmi karma; अपि – also; ज्ञानेन – by Knowledge; नश्यति – is destroyed; किञ्च – also; आगामि-कर्मणां – of āgāmi karmas; नलिनीदलगतजलवत् – like the water on the lotus leaf; ज्ञानिनां – for the wise man; सम्बन्धः – relation; न अस्ति – is not there

The āgāmi karma is also destroyed by Knowledge and the wise man is not affected by it, as a lotus leaf is not affected by the water on it.

The sañcita karma is destroyed by Knowledge and the wise man is not reborn. The prārabdha karma too, does not affect him, as he has no identification with the body. But what about the actions done in the present? Would he not have to enjoy or suffer their results here or hereafter? Since the very notion of doership dies, there remains none to enjoy or suffer the results of actions done even in the present. Remaining in the midst of actions, he is still totally untouched by them, like the lotus leaf in water. The lotus leaf is born in water, remains in water and dies there, yet it never gets wet.

Once Śrī Buddha was abused while he was asking for alms. The disciple got angry and asked Śrī Buddha, "Shall I give him a piece of my mind?" Śrī Buddha said, "If you have taken anything, you have to return it. Since I have not taken anything, I do not have to give back anything."

***

But actions must have results. If they do not go to the wise man, who gets them? It is explained thus.

किञ्च ये ज्ञानिनं स्तुवन्ति भजन्ति अर्चयन्ति तान्प्रति ज्ञानिकृतं
आगामि पुण्यं गच्छति।
ये ज्ञानिनं निन्दन्ति द्विषन्ति दुःखप्रदानं कुर्वन्ति तान्प्रति
ज्ञानिकृतं सर्वमागामि क्रियमाणं यदवाच्यं कर्म पापात्मकं
तद् गच्छति। सुहृदः पुण्यकृत्यं दुर्हृदः पापकृत्यं गह्णन्ति इति।।

*kiñca ye jñāninaṁ stuvanti bhajanti arcayanti*
*tānprati jñānikṛtam āgāmi puṇyaṁ gacchati,*
*ye jñāninaṁ nindanti dviṣanti duḥkha-pradānaṁ*
*kurvanti tānprati jñānikṛtaṁ sarvam-āgāmi*
*kriyamāṇaṁ yadavācyaṁ karma pāpātmakaṁ*
*tadgacchati, suhṛdaḥ puṇyakṛtyaṁ durhṛdaḥ pāpakṛtyaṁ*
*gṛhṇanti iti.*

किञ्च – further; ये – those; ज्ञानिनं – the wise man; स्तुवन्ति – praise; भजन्ति – serve; अर्चयन्ति – worship; तान् प्रति – to them; ज्ञानिकृतं – done by the wise man; आगामि – āgāmi; पुण्यं – the results of good actions; गच्छति – goes; ये – those; ज्ञानिनं – wise man; निन्दन्ति – criticise; द्विषन्ति – hate; दुःखप्रदानं कुर्वन्ति – give pain; तान् प्रति – to them; ज्ञानिकृतं – done by the wise man; आगामि क्रियमाणं – āgāmi karma; यत् – which; अवाच्यं – not praiseworthy; कर्म – actions; पापात्मकं – sinful; तद् – that; गच्छति - goes; सुहृदः – friends; पुण्यकृत्यं – meritorious actions; दुर्हृदः – enemies; पापकृत्यं – demeritorious actions; गृह्णन्ति – take; इति – thus

Further, to those who praise, serve and worship the wise man, go the results of the good actions done by the wise man. To those who criticise, hate or cause pain to the wise man go the results of all unpraiseworthy and sinful actions done by the wise.

Friends take the meritorious results and enemies the demeritorious results. Every action has two sides, if its good effects, by far override the bad, we call it a good action. The doctor operates on the patient and causes him pain and the relatives tension, yet it is a good action. When the bad effects dominate, it is a bad action. The wise man's actions always spring from good intentions, but they can have bad effects also. Since the wise man is not the enjoyer or sufferer of the good or bad results, whom do they go to? It is said that the good results go to those who love him and the bad to those who hate him. The wise man himself, does not will that the results go to any particular person. The actions done by him are the will of the Lord or the demand of the Totality. The results are therefore, distributed according to His will or the will of the Totality. The mind of one who loves and worships the wise man is purified and therefore, attracts the results of good actions. The mind of one who criticises and hates is negative and therefore, attracts the results of bad actions.

One who has value for Knowledge and ideals, whose mind is pure and subtle, recognises the greatness of the wise man. They revere and serve him not for getting merits but for the supreme Knowledge or out of gratitude, for having received it or out of gratitude for the transformation in their lives. Some look at the wise man from the standpoint of their ignorance and superimpose their own prejudices on him. Some go to him with expectations and if they are not fulfilled, criticise him. Some with evil minds, hate anyone who is good and even try to harm him. The wise man however, is equal and unbiased to the one who loves him and the one who hates him.

If we are not able to see greatness in the wise man and are not able to worship him, we must at least stay away from him and not criticise him or create dislike and hate for him as this can bring about our own downfall. The examples of Rāvaṇa, Kaṁsa and such demonic natured ones who criticised the Lord are well known in Hindu scriptures.

# Result of Self-knowledge

The result of Self-knowledge is summarised by quotes from the Śruti and Smṛti in the concluding words of the text.

तथा चात्मवित्संसारं तीर्त्वा ब्रह्मानन्दमिहैव प्राप्नोति।
तरति शोकमात्मवित् इति श्रुतेः।
तनुं त्यजतु वा काश्यां श्वपचस्य गृहेऽथ वा।
ज्ञानसंप्राप्तिसमये मुक्तोऽसौ विगताशयः। इति स्मृतेश्च।।

*tathā cātmavit-saṁsāraṁ tīrtvā brahmānandam-*
*ihaiva prāpnoti, tarati śokam-ātmavit iti śruteḥ,*
*tanuṁ tyajatu vā kāśyāṁ śvapacasya gṛhe'tha vā,*
*jñāna-saṁprāpti-samaye mukto'sau vigatāśayaḥ, iti smṛteśca.*

तथा – thus; च – and; आत्मवित् – the knower of the Self; संसारं – saṁsāra; तीर्त्वा – having crossed; ब्रह्मानन्दम् – supreme Bliss; इह – here; एव – alone; प्राप्नोति – gains; तरति – crosses; शोकम् – sorrow; आत्मवित् – knower of the Self; इति – thus; श्रुतेः – the Śruti says; तनुं – body; त्यजतु – may it be given up; वा – or; काश्यां – in Kāśī; श्वपचस्य – of a dog eater; गृहे – in the house; अथवा – or; ज्ञानसंप्राप्तिसमये – at the time of attaining Knowledge; मुक्तः – Liberated; असौ – he; विगताशयः – free from the results of actions; इति – thus; स्मृतेः च – and the Smṛti says

Thus the knower of the Self, having crossed saṁsāra, attains supreme Bliss here itself. The Śruti affirms – the knower of the Self goes beyond all sorrow. Let the wise man cast off his body in Kāśī or in the house of a dog-eater (it is immaterial because) at the time of gaining Knowledge (itself) he is Liberated, being freed from all the results of his actions. So assert the Smṛtis too.

That which is forever changing is called saṁsāra (saṁsarati iti saṁsāra). The entire realm of time, space and objects is saṁsāra. Limitations cause sorrow. The knower of the Self goes beyond the limitations of time, space and objects and therefore, attains infinity, which is supreme Bliss. The knower of an object does not become the object. For example, the one who knows a tree does not become a tree. But the knower of the Self (Truth) becomes the Truth itself. (brahmavid brahmaiva bhavati). In reality, there is no becoming. He only comes to realise that he was always of the nature of supreme Bliss, even while in ignorance.

*Chāndogya Upaniṣad*, chapter 7 narrates how Sage Nārada approaches the Sanat Kumāras and seeks that Knowledge by which one can cross over all sorrows. When asked to list what he already knew, he enumerates all that he has mastered including all the sciences, arts, social sciences and politics.

The Guru then teaches him Self-knowledge, concluding that only the knower of the Self crosses over grief (tarati śokam ātmavit). We too, having studied many subjects, have not got over sorrow, tension and agitations. Ignorant of the Self, we seek various worldly ways of getting rid of sorrow and so do not succeed.

We are afraid of death and pray for a good death. Some wish to die in sleep, others when their body is healthy and when they are engaged in activity and yet others hope to give up the body remembering the Lord. Some believe in certain days, times and places as auspicious and think that one who dies then will attain a good birth, hereafter or get liberated. Yet others believe that the place from where the subtle body leaves the gross body would decide the course of the future of the individual. If the subtle body leaves through the top of the head, then one attains Liberation. Bhīṣma Pitāmaha waited for the auspicious uttarāyaṇa time for leaving his body. It is said that one who dies in Kāśī gets liberated. Kāśī is on the banks of the holy river Ganga where Lord Viśvanātha, (Śiva) resides. Just before a person dies, the Lord Himself is believed to give him the tāraka mantra (liberating mantra), chanting which the person leaves his body and gets liberated. One with faith would naturally live a pious life and spend his days in Kāśī in the remembrance of the Lord and therefore, when he does chanting of His name, he gets liberated as our mind gets affected by the environment in which we live.

As far as the wise man is concerned, he is already Liberated even before the time of death. Therefore, it is immaterial under what circumstance or condition of the body, the time or the place he leaves the mortal body. He may do so even in a dog-eater's house. (A dog is the best friend of man. He serves his master with faith. One who eats a dog is therefore, said to be the worst of men). He may pass away while in coma or while in meditation. He was Liberated while living in the body (Jīvanmukta). Now he is said to be Liberated without body (Videhamukta). This distinction is purely from the standpoint of the ignorant man whose attention is on his body.

***

इति तत्त्वबोधप्रकरणं समाप्तम्।।

*iti tattvabodha-prakaraṇaṁ samāptam.*

इति – thus; तत्त्वबोधप्रकरणं – the prakaraṇa called *Tattvabodha*; समाप्तम् – ends

Thus ends the prākaraṇa called *Tattvabodha*.

Bhagavān Ādi Śaṅkarācārya has written a wide range of literature which appeals to people of various ages, education and levels of evolution. He has written commentaries on the prasthāna trayī (the *Brahma Sūtra*, the *Gītā*, and the Upaniṣads), various prākaraṇa granthas (introductory texts), stotrams (hymns in praise of the Lord) and many other texts.

In *Tattvabodha*, he starts with qualifications of the student, continues with the discussion of the jīva (individual), jagat (world) and Īśvara (the Creator) and establishes their essential identity. He concludes with the description of the Realised Master. The entire subject matter of Vedānta is covered in this simple text. Even though it is a prākaraṇa grantha meant for the beginner, if a sincere seeker reflects and meditates on its words, he could get established in his own Self. It also helps the study of other texts of Vedānta. May all be benefitted by it.

Om tat sat